THE NEW GOLD RUSH - REAL ESTATE

Capitalist Series

A proven framework to retire in 10 years with the assistance of the IRS and prudent real estate initiatives!

Mark P.
Mac Kenzie
Real Estate Planner®

www.TheNewGoldRush.biz

MARK MACKENZIE®

REAL ESTATE PLANNING

This book is sold with the understanding that the author is not rendering financial, accounting, or legal services. Each scenario is unique; questions pertaining to finance, accounting, or the practice of law should be directed to the appropriate professional.

DEDICATION

This is dedicated to the individuals that know they deserve more success than they are currently receiving in both their finances and most importantly their lives. My hope is that this framework will be a catalyst and a foundation for you to begin to take massive action to achieve all of your dreams.

ACKNOWLEDGEMENTS

This book is a product of my environment. They say that you are most like the people that you surround yourself with. If this is the case, then I am truly fortunate and blessed to have several incredible people in my life that have made this book a reality.

My Dad, who has since passed on, has left me and others who he touched with a legacy of faith, hope, and courage. He taught me to never, ever, give up.

My Mom, you have been more of a support system for me than you will ever know. I have enjoyed being able to share with you both my triumphs and challenges along the road. You continue to set an example for me with your courage and passion for life.

My brothers Kevin and Bruce, you have always been there to help whenever I asked; and most importantly have always been there to share a laugh.

To Sarah for putting up with this project and for believing in me and us.

To Jason and Matt for being an inspiration for me; your successes have driven me to excel.

Mary Dougherty for your knowledge, time, and enthusiasm; you have done more to push this project forward than you realize. You are truly a beautiful person.

Jeff Colling with Colling Photography and Lori Meisner Cleland with Visage Creative Business Services, for understanding my vision for the book cover and making it happen. You have both been true professionals and wonderful to work with.

Anthony Robbins for helping me establish my psychological roadmap and opening my eyes to a much brighter future than I would have ever thought possible.

AUTHOR'S NOTE

This book is designed as a psychological and strategic roadmap for individuals, regardless of their current financial status, who desire to achieve financial independence in 10 years with the assistance of the IRS and proven real estate initiatives.

It was written out of a necessity to assist individuals to make prudent decisions not only when investing and holding real estate but also about managing the equity in their own personal residences. There have been volumes written about techniques and opportunities for legendary real estate investing, but none of them work for everybody all of the time like this framework does.

As with any venture, a certain blend of inspiration mixed with perspiration will yield the best results; this book provides both for you. All the knowledge in the world will not produce anything unless that knowledge is put into motion and action.

Regardless of where you are in your life and the struggles you may be going through, your financial life can be turned around and transformed into one of freedom and abundance.

CONTENTS

PART ONE
THE PSYCHOLOGY
IF YOU CAN CONCEIVE IT YOU CAN ACHIEVE IT

PART TWO
THE PLAN
BUILDING YOUR EMPIRE

PART THREE
THE MONEY
FUNDING THE CAPITAL PROJECT

PART FOUR
THE TIME
YOUR MOST PRECIOUS RESOURCE

APPENDIX

PART ONE

THE PSYCHOLOGY

IF YOU CAN CONCEIVE IT YOU CAN ACHIEVE IT

CHAPTER 1
YOU DECIDE

> *"Insanity: doing the same thing over and over again and expecting different results."*
>
> *Albert Einstein*

This book is not intended to sell you on financial independence; financial independence is a commodity that sells itself. Instead the mission of this book is to illuminate a road map for you, a road map that leads from debt, poverty, and dependence, to abundance, wealth, and independence. It is a road map that each and every individual can follow, regardless of their current circumstances or financial situation.

The secret to financial success is not how much money you make, or how much money you save; in fact, we are currently surrounded by literally hundreds of thousands, perhaps even millions of these types of individuals that followed that path to financial oblivion and distress. The road map to financial independence is littered with carcasses of individuals that had good jobs and that made and saved a significant amount of money. But because these individuals did not invest prudently, they continue to pay too much in tax, and they will never be able to retire or become financially independent.

The key to financial success is to take advantage of two very powerful financial tools, leverage and tax loopholes. And the only medium to put to use these financial tools is through real estate and the careful and prudent acquisition of properties and the management of their equity.

The time period that we are now in is going to be one of the most ballistic wealth accumulation periods since the gold rush of 1849. Today's gold rush, real estate, is being driven by two forces: an increase in real estate education and awareness, and the correction of the stock market at the turn of the millennium.

THE NEW GOLD RUSH

The real gold rush began in San Francisco in 1848; it was one of the most incredible adventures the world had ever seen. By 1849, thanks to an official statement by President James Polk, word had spread back East about the opportunities for fortune seekers. Gold fever had exploded and was now an absolute epidemic. Unfortunately for many, by mid 1849 most of the gold had been mined and more and more Easterners and foreigners were still continuing to make the trip West in search of wealth and financial independence. The scarcity of gold and the insurgence of fortune seekers led to massive fortunes for some and a catastrophe for other gold miners and their families.

The market for single family houses, today's equivalent of gold, is also limited to an extent. The production of single family houses is limited purely because of the slowly growing scarcity of desirable land that is available for development. You have probably noticed this trend where you live if you reside near a thriving city or along the coast. Places like Cape Cod, Massachusetts and Newport, Rhode Island, just to name a couple of cities from "my neck of the woods," have literally exhausted the amount of land they have available to develop.

Combining this trickling yet growing scarcity of land with an ever-increasing demand for housing, due to the swelling national population and flood of immigrants, you have in your hands a very valuable commodity, single family houses. It is not at all surprising that the price of single family houses has consistently been on the rise since 1940.

In fact, you don't have to go back too far in United States history to see how the price of land has exploded in value through the years. The 600 million acre acquisition of the Louisiana Territory by President Thomas Jefferson in 1803 was purchased from France for only $15 million. This equates to a bargain-price of 2.5 cents an acre!

The Alaskan Territory, 375 million acres, was acquired during President Andrew Johnson's term in 1867 from Russia for $7.2 million. This transaction equated to a monumental acquisition of just 2 cents an acre!

Despite skeptics that held the belief that the Louisiana Purchase was unconstitutional and imprudent, or those that called the acquisition of the Alaskan Territory, by the then Secretary of State William H. Seward, as "Seward's Folly," we can now see very clearly that these acquisitions were the right thing to do.

Fast-forwarding to today's landscape, it should be no surprise that the individuals that choose to dig for gold and acquire and hold real estate will become wealthy. Unlike the gold rush, however, any person that wants to mine and acquire properties will find riches. Those that choose not to acquire today's form of gold, single family houses, will continue to live their lives as they have done; and they will continue to receive the same results.

Most people at some point in their lives will buy a home; why not more than one? A house is the best investment a person will ever make in their lifetime in terms of capital growth, *and* in most instances, it provides the largest annual tax write-off an individual will have. It is not as if this framework is about acquiring a foreign commodity like coconuts from Indonesia; we are talking real estate, land, houses. It is that simple; it is your decision.

THE INFORMATION AGE

"Every now and then a man's mind is stretched by a new idea and never shrinks back to its original proportion."

Oliver Wendell Holmes Jr.

After reading this book you will have every piece of information made available to you. The framework will be illustrated, the foundation will be laid, the road map will be drawn, and there will be an "x" on the map; and all you have to do is take action.

Think about it; all of this powerful wealth-building information being given to you for the cost of a couple cups of coffee at the local corner Starbucks. It is truly amazing; we live in the most unbelievable time in our history, the information age. It is an age where information is being exchanged so quickly that often times the morning paper is old news because by the time you get it you have already read about the event on the internet at your office, heard it on talk radio on your way home from work, or seen it on NBC news after your dinner.

We live in a time according to the Wall Street proverb where we, "buy on the rumor, sell on the news." Or more recently thanks to some crooked CEO's and bookkeepers, we now are forced to, "sell on the rumor."

Business is moving at such a rapid pace that once we think we know what to do, the strategy has already changed and we are left running late and without a date for the high school prom.

FOOL'S GOLD

"In a time of turbulence and change, it is more true than ever that knowledge is power."

John F. Kennedy

So what is the solution to today's investing quagmire? An understanding of the market, an understanding of what and who it is you are actually investing your money in or with; none of the above? Today's investors have been burned and are uncertain as to where to turn to with their money and where to grow it safely.

Let's face it, we are in the middle of a drastically changing investment landscape. Never before have so many people turned to real estate for their investments. And never before, because of a lack of education, have so many people been getting burned and borderline terrorized with their real estate investments. There is absolutely no framework or precedent that has been established to assist and advise people on how to prudently and effectively invest their money in real estate. There have been plenty of chapters and books written on opportunities and borderline biblical real estate dealings, but there is an anemic amount of information on sound and prudent real estate principals and investment structures for those of you who don't want to speculate in the foreclosure market or on other risky investments, or those of you that don't want to quit your day job. The reality is that there are too many real estate investors or advisors teaching or advising without a syllabus or a framework. Many of these teachers or professionals that you see on TV or read about in their books might as well be telling you to go get a shovel and a pan and start mining for gold in the Colorado River. Their advice is not going to work for *everybody all* of the time.

Don't misunderstand, there are opportunities to successfully speculate in real estate. There are opportunities to acquire properties at a discount. There are opportunities to acquire properties with no-money down. *Some* of these concepts will work for a *small* percentage of the population *some* of the time. This book explains concepts that *will* work for *all* of us *all* of the time.

The tragic reality of today's real estate market is that these types of discount or no-money down "deals" are becoming in short supply because of the exposure they receive; it is simple economics. Consistent supply with an increase in demand lends itself to less and less desirable property acquisitions for ordinary people with full-time jobs and careers.

When was the last time you turned on the television and you *didn't* see one of these types of speculative real estate infomercials? Or perhaps you have already even bought one of these products only to be disappointed when you didn't accumulate massive amounts of wealth and passive cash flow in nine months. The bottom line is that if these types of methods and strategies worked *all* the time then we would *all* be rich, retired, and on late night TV giving our testimonials. But unfortunately we are not.

Even if these "deals" were in abundance, you still would not need to pursue them based on the investment campaign that is detailed in this book.

A PRUDENT INITIATIVE

"To avoid criticism, do nothing, say nothing, be nothing."

Elbert Hubbard

The objective of this book is to provide you with a framework or a plan that *will* work for *everybody all* of the time, a framework that will transcend both geography and generations. It is a proven initiative to retire in 10 years with the assistance of the IRS and prudent real estate initiatives.

The only obstacle stopping you from completing this framework may be the criticism or *concern* you receive from your *loving* friends or family. Do not let these individuals deter you from your objective. A good rule of thumb is to take advice only from people who have what you want or who are where you want to be. So unless one of these *concerned* family members owns multiple properties or is independently wealthy through their own doing, you should probably seek a second opinion.

YOU DECIDE

> *"It's not that some people have willpower and some don't. It's that some people are ready to change and others are not."*
>
> *James Gordon, M.D.*

This leads us to a very important crossroad. You, and only you, need to make a decision at the end of this book as to whether or not you are going to take action. At the completion of this book you will have an empowered psychology, a detailed and proven plan, a strategy to fund the capital project, and a plan to leverage your time to see the plan through so you don't have to quit your day job, yet. There are no *reasons* that would support your not wanting to move forward if you do truly want a better life for yourself and your family. In fact, those people that are not getting on with their lives and becoming financially independent are becoming more and more in the minority; it is not just your imagination.

We are literally surrounded by millionaires; some estimates show over 3.5 million people in America are millionaires. According to the Texas Banking Association 1 out of every 36 workers in America is a millionaire.

We have at our fingertips information that will provide us with financial abundance and independence for the rest of our lives. We can go to a library or bookstore or on the internet in our own home and read about any number of self-made multi-millionaires or even billionaires, people like Rockefeller, Getty, Carnegie, Gates, Buffet, and even Trump. We can read about these people every day. We can learn what their thought sequences were, and see how these thought sequences led to their belief systems, and how these belief systems led to their actions that in turn reaped their failures as well as successes, but ultimately and most importantly, their destiny.

So if you have this information, what is the decision *you're* making that is stopping you from achieving this same level of financial abundance, or at the least, financial independence? Is it your psychology? Do you think you are not deserving of the financial rewards? Maybe your *reason* for not taking action is your lack of a definitive plan, or that you don't have any money or credit? Perhaps you don't have the time to see the framework through. Or maybe your *reason* is a fine and homemade self-pity recipe of all four of these ingredients? Whatever your *reason*, this book provides you with the answer to all four of these *excuses* you have about not getting on with your life, the life that you were meant to live.

You see, whether or not you are aware of it, you do make a decision about what your destiny is going to be. Whether or not you will acknowledge it, you are where you are in life because of the decisions *you* have made. Take responsibility for those decisions.

It is very simple, either you decide to work towards your goal or you don't. For most people it is a subconscious decision that is layered so deep with excuses and reasons as to why they can't or won't do something, that they don't let even one thought translate into the smallest of actions that could potentially propel them into creating a desired habit and eventually a character trait and ultimately their triumphant destiny.

Financial abundance and independence, for a multitude of reasons, must first be achieved in your mind before it can be done in the real world. You must vividly see, feel, and experience the emotions of this type of success in your mind before you will experience and attract these same emotions and feelings in reality.

THE BENEFITS OF REAL ESTATE

> *"Give me a lever and a place to stand, and I will move the world."*
>
> *Archimedes*

Real Estate is *the* vehicle that you will use to achieve financial abundance. Real Estate is a commodity that has massive potential and numerous safeguards that make it a very magnetic investment. Examples of these benefits include leverage, appreciation, legal tax savings, cash flow, and equity build-up or principal reduction. The safeguards are property inspections, appraisals, homeowner's associations, homeowner's insurance, home warranties, a fairly liquid resale market, and equity resources such as lines of credit or refinancing techniques. And best of all, it is "real" as the name implies. It is not fabricated, doctored, or embellished like many of the public companies we see in the NASDAQ or NYSE.

Leverage has really two meanings when you talk about investing in real estate. First, clearly you can leverage your investment so that you can acquire an asset or property with only ten, five, three, or in some cases zero percent down. The second part of leverage is that you are able to leverage your time and money into an investment or income property by having a tenant help you take care of the property while at the same time making your mortgage payments for you. As Don Marquis once said, "when a man tells you that he got rich through hard work, ask him: Whose?" Real estate investing is your opportunity to get rich through the hard work of your tenants.

According to the OFHEO, (Office of Federal Housing Enterprise Oversight) real estate, in particular residential real estate, has been appreciating nationally at an eight percent clip since 1980.

Real estate also provides massive tax savings in the form of not just cost of business write-offs but also the depreciation of the property.

By structuring the financing of the property prudently, you are able to generate passive cash flow on a monthly basis.

Finally, the longer you hold onto the property, the more equity you are able to build up, not just via the appreciation, but also monthly principal payments you or preferably your tenant makes on the mortgage.

Property inspections allow you to inspect the property inside and out before you buy it. So if there is an item that is damaged, not working, or an item that is at risk of not working, you can ask for it to be repaired or replaced, or you can walk from the deal altogether.

An appraisal is a tool that is used to assure you and the lender that you are not paying more than fair market value for the property.

Homeowner's associations insure the property and neighborhood are being kept up in good aesthetic standing. They prevent cars and couches from ending up in the front yard.

Homeowner's insurance protects you from property damage, loss, or repairs.

Home warranty plans work as an "insurance policy" to hedge your risk on unforeseen and expensive repairs that will at some point arise during the time you own the property.

In addition, properties at a median value are in a fairly liquid market, and equity resources such as lines of credit and refinancing techniques allow this "market" to become even more liquid.

All of these unique and powerful tools will be elaborated on throughout this book; for now, know that they are there, they are incredibly powerful, and they are unique to real estate investing only.

As you navigate through this book you will be convinced that what you will learn is the most substantiated, sound, and powerful initiative for achieving your financial independence with the least amount of financial exposure and in the shortest amount of time possible.

The framework is very clear and concise. And it leaves it up to you to decide if you want to take action and achieve the desired results outlined here; or if you want to have read this book for enjoyment purposes only, and consciously decide that you don't want to massively improve your finances or any other part of your life. It *is your* choice. I can assure you that for whatever excuse or reason that may be going through your mind right now as to why you can't do what this book advises you to do, there is at *least* one other person that has been in your same circumstances, if not worse, and has since massively transformed his or her life based on these sound principles and initiatives.

Real Estate has the potential to provide you with tremendous returns on your investment and at the same time contribute massive tax benefits to your bottom line. No other investment can match the advantages of real estate if it is used for its highest and best use. But like everything else in life, you must have a foundation and a plan from which you can build. This book will very clearly illustrate the foundation and the plan for you; there is no guesswork, fortunate timing, massive financial exposure or luck involved. All you have to do is decide if you want to follow the road map and get on the fast lane to financial independence and abundance or stay with the plan you have now, if you even have one.

As you progress into Part Two, Three, and Four of this book understand that the hypothetical and conservative examples are just that, hypothetical and conservative examples. The results that you experience with this plan and the decisions that you make will lend themselves to varying wealth accumulation and tax advantages. Because the real estate market is so diverse across our great country, the results will be significantly different for someone living in Newport, Rhode Island compared to somebody living in Oklahoma City, Oklahoma. But the results *will* be consistent in that both of these individuals will be more financially independent than if they had not taken action.

Real estate is truly a very simple investment if you follow a very simple plan. Or it can be very complicated and perhaps even disastrous if you don't. But clearly there is an incredible amount of opportunity by using real estate as an investment.

ALTERNATIVES?

> *"When you find that you are on the side of the majority, it is time to reform."*
>
> *Mark Twain*

So if after reading this book, from cover to cover, you decide that this framework is not for you, what are your alternatives? Can you afford *not* to follow the investment framework? The stock market, social security, and your savings accounts have all proven that they fall short of the mark.

The equity or stock market and your retirement plan "formerly known as 401K," now 201K; may not be the most secure method for you to plan for retirement. We have learned that where there is smoke there is a bonfire, of financial documents. Here are a couple of reasons why the stock market pales in comparison to real estate.

First, the books and the crooks: you don't know what or who you are *really* investing in. The harsh reality of today's equities market is that it is ultra-competitive, and it is driven exclusively by the numbers; it is absolutely unforgiving. Because shareholders and the directors of publicly held companies have a temperament and a need to continually grow, the result is a win and profit at all costs mentality. The repercussion to shareholders is an unstable investment medium that has made many of us to look like the North end of a South bound horse. This is not what you want to base your retirement and financial well-being on.

If you had bought $1,000 of WorldCom stock one year ago you would have less than $5 left. A $1,000 investment in Enron would leave you with $16.50. And a $1,000 dumped into Nortel stock one year ago would now be worth $49.00. On the other hand if you had bought a $1,000 worth of Budweiser, the beer not the stock, and recycled the five cent cans you would have $113. This is more than the three companies combined! This example is not only intended to be funny, but to also prove a point. The equities market presents some serious concerns.

Second, the stock market does not provide a hedge against inflation like real estate does. Regardless of the economic climate in the Dow or NASDAQ, inflation is unforgiving; it continues to grow.

And third, and unfortunately, today's economy is directly wired into homeland security. All it takes is one terrorist attack to turn the market inside-out and wipe out your portfolio. Homeland security is directly wired into your financial security.

Social Security, now known to many people in the current work force as Social *Insecurity,* is not going to be able to benefit most of us unless there are *major* and *expensive* reforms done. According to the Social Security Administration, the current financial problems will not affect today's retirees or near retirees, but they will have borderline catastrophic effects for those in their 20's and 30's.

By the year 2042 the Social Security Administration expects a reduction of benefits by 27 percent with a possibility of continuing reductions for the years moving forward. The cause is that the worker-to-beneficiary ratio that was once 16-to-1 in 1950; has fallen to 3.3-to-1 today. Within 40 years they expect the worker-to-beneficiary ratio will be 2-to-1. At this ratio, there will clearly not be enough people in the work force to pay for the benefits at current tax rates.

These statistics mean two things for you. First, there is a strong likelihood that when and *if* you retire, your social security benefits will be insignificant or ineffective at best. And, second, you should not be surprised if in the near future you begin to have more money withdrawn from *your* paycheck to help resolve and fund this eminent social security debacle.

Perhaps you plan on *saving* your way to retirement and financial independence. Good luck. A combination of historic annual inflation and *relatively* weak interest rates on savings accounts makes these type of accounts at best, a savings account not a growth account, and at worst a losing account due to inflation.

What do all three of these *plans* have in common? They all are suspect and they all take a *long* time. Let's face it; the long way is the wrong way. We are in the eye of the perfect storm right now; the vast majority of Americans have very serious financial problems, and we need very serious and effective solutions to solve these problems. Now is not the time for hope; it is a time for action.

According to the U.S. Department of Human Resources the *median* income of a 65-year old American is less than $13,000 *annually*. The average American aged 65, has less than $2,500 in the bank! And not surprisingly, only two percent of these 65-year olds are financially independent.

What is even worse, the trend is not just for the aged but for people still in the workforce. According to an article in the Associated Press, "most" of the upper-income households in America had problems paying their "necessary" bills.

Clearly, your best bet for financial success is to determine what the masses are doing, and do the opposite! This is what this book is about, how to begin playing the financial game at a higher level, at a major league level, so that the decisions you make can begin to have a profound and powerful impact on your financial life. The bottom line is that you can't afford *not* to take action on this framework.

A BIG ENOUGH "WHY?"

"Each man the architect of his own fate."

Appius Claudius

So now we know what works and what doesn't work. Now you have to determine *why* you should take action on *this* framework. As Gary Keller states in his book *The Millionaire Real Estate Agent,* you need to give yourself a big enough "why?" Determine for yourself why financial freedom and abundance is *critical* if not *essential* for your livelihood. Is it so you can quit your job, buy a bigger home, a nicer car, fund your kid's college education, or live the life you always imagined?

Once *you* find the answer to *your* "why," you can determine what actions need to be taken and what price needs to be paid. Once you know this, every obstacle will be able to be overcome in your quest to achieve your goal.

If you can determine *why* it is important to you and then come to a conclusion about what price needs to be paid to accomplish the objective, you can then go pay the price.

Think of it as a plane ticket; if you want to fly from New York to Los Angeles, you are going to need to buy a plane ticket, for a price. The same is true for this investment framework; if you want to get from where you are now, financial dependence, to financial independence and abundance; you are going to have to pay a price. It is up to you to determine what you are willing to pay. If you have a big enough why, then you have a blank check to make it happen. Don't leave it up to chance; make a choice.

If you want to own your own business, work for yourself, and be retired in 10 years, like most Americans do, then this framework is your answer.

So as you navigate through this book and this information, remind yourself that is your, and only your, decision to make this plan happen. Either you plan for your future, or somebody else will have a plan for you in theirs.

> *"Because you are in control of your life, don't ever forget that. You are what you are because of the conscious and subconscious choices you have made."*
>
> *Barbara Hall*

POINTS TO REMEMBER: YOU DECIDE

1.) The market for single family houses, today's equivalent of gold, is also limited, to an extent. The production of single family houses is limited purely because of the slowly growing scarcity of desirable land that is available to be developed.

2.) The demand for single family houses is increasing every day due to the increase in population growth. This is a trend that will continue for many years moving forward.

3.) After reading this book you will have every piece of information made available to you. The framework will be illustrated, the foundation will be laid, the road map will be drawn, there will be an "x" on the map, and all you have to do is take action.

4.) Never before, because of a lack of knowledge, have so many people been getting burned and borderline terrorized with their real estate investments.

5.) The purpose of this book is to provide you with a framework or a plan that *will* work for *everybody all* of the time.

6.) It is your decision as to whether or not you choose to act on the framework that this book will teach you. No one else can decide for you. The reality is that you make a decision either way. Either you decide to continue what you have been doing or you decide to make a change.

7.) Real Estate is a commodity that has massive potential and numerous safeguards that make it a very magnetic investment. Examples of these benefits include leverage, appreciation, legal tax savings, cash flow, and equity build-up or principal reduction. The safeguards are property inspections, appraisals, homeowner's associations, homeowner's insurance, home warranties, a fairly liquid resale market, and equity resources such as lines of credit or refinancing techniques. And best of all, it is "real" as the name implies.

8.) What you will learn is the most substantiated, sound, and powerful initiative for achieving your financial independence with the least amount of financial exposure and in the shortest amount of time possible.

9.) Give yourself a big enough "why?" Once *you* find the answer to *your* "why," any action can be taken, and every obstacle can be overcome in your quest to achieve your goal.

CHAPTER 2
CREATE A BELIEF SYSTEM

> *"Whether you think you can or you think you can't, you're right."*
>
> *Henry Ford*

A SELF-FULFILLING PROPHECY

> *"I am a great believer in luck, and I find the harder I work, the more I have of it."*
>
> *Thomas Jefferson*

In 1932 Henry Ford was responsible for bringing this saying to light when he and his team were putting together the first ever V-8 Ford car. Despite an overwhelming sentiment that it was "impossible" to build this type of engine, Ford persisted, and not surprisingly, accomplished the "impossible" feat.

It is very simple, if you truly believe you can do something, you will take the necessary actions matched with an unrelenting persistence, and you *will* accomplish anything. If you don't believe you can do something, you won't attempt it or take the required action, and clearly you won't accomplish the desired result.

This same law applies to the investing framework explained in this book. If you believe in the strategy, and you are absolutely convinced you can achieve the desired result, you will. If you have the required fortitude matched with the appropriate belief system, you can and will accomplish the goal, regardless of what obstacles you may have to overcome along the way. Vacancies, repairs, and late payments will all seem like *minor* inconveniences that will have no negative effect on you as you move steadfast and with resolve towards your goal.

SHORT-TERM LOSSES

> *"Anyone who has never made a mistake has never tried anything new."*
>
> *Albert Einstein*

Let me say this now; if you have not already experienced it for yourself first hand, regardless of how well you plan and prepare for an investment or acquisition, it is not unusual for people to lose money, short-term, in real estate investments. You need to be aware, understand, and plan accordingly for the possibility of a short-term "loss."

The reality though is that money is nothing more than a tool to be used to get you where you want go with your life. What money does is allow you to buy time, or stated differently, when we have money, we can choose what we want to do with our time instead of giving our time to a boss. The more money we have, the less we have to work, the more we can get other people to do the things we don't want to do. The loss of money is nothing to get emotional about; the conservation or hording of it is. There is an abundance of money all around us. It permeates into our lives. The world will never run out of money. Your job is to put your money to work to make more of it so that eventually *you* don't have to work, and your money can continue to proliferate. So as the saying goes, if you don't use it, you *will* lose it.

It is true, real estate investing is not all blue sky and green grass; there are tenants, toilets, and risks involved. Tenants are people; they make mistakes, lose jobs, and go through divorces, just like you or I. Toilets have moving parts and they can break, overflow, and flood your home. And like every other investment, there is a direct correlation between risk and reward; the greater the risk, the greater the reward. Fortunately, this framework provides a very strong hedge that allows you to massively reduce your financial exposure and risk for your real estate investments.

It is important to disclose these variables because there must be an understanding that bad things do happen to good people. And that if you are aware of this possibility going into this endeavor, you will be much more prepared to psychologically "weather the storm" when you experience short-term obstacles. This understanding has a profound significance on helping you to establish and maintain a strong resolve.

YOU GOT TO BELIEVE!

> *"In actual life every great enterprise begins with and takes its first forward step in faith."*
>
> *Frederich von Schlegel*

The investing campaign that you are about to embark upon must begin in your mind first. Before you can achieve anything physically, you must accomplish the goal in your mind first. Whether you believe you can do something or you don't, you're right. It is essential that you change your paradigms in order to achieve great success. You must change the way your beliefs construct you.

If you control what you think, you control your actions, and ultimately your destiny. By changing your beliefs you can experience real changes or results in your life. This is absolutely true not only in real estate investing but in other aspects of life as well.

Take a look at America's obsession with fitness. The only reason people drive themselves to the gym and put themselves through a relentless workout is to generate results. Most people don't enjoy the activity of working out because they like to sweat or have the *challenge* for the next week of performing necessary daily functions because of muscle soreness. But somehow, people are able to reframe the workout because they like to feel fit and healthy and they want to look great. If it were scientifically possible, people would rather pop a pill to get a toned and firm physique. And because there is not a pill available that will generate the desired results, people have had to resort to putting in the time and energy to *hopefully* create the body they desire.

To make it through an effective workout you need to have confidence or a belief that in the end, there is going to be a pay off. It is called delayed gratification. The investing mentality is really no different. There are no short cuts or pills or ways to cheat if you really want life lasting results.

You must believe that by putting yourself through this investment framework you will obtain the results that you desire. In some respects it is similar to a leap of faith; realize that the world has a way of rewarding those who have a desire to take action and to achieve something. It is a universal law, whatever you put into something, you will get out of it. If you truly believe in something with your mind, body, and spirit you will be able to virtually will it to happen.

A PASSIONATE INTENSITY

> *"I am the greatest.*
> *I said that even before I knew I was.*
> *Don't tell me I can't do something.*
> *Don't tell me it's impossible.*
> *Don't tell me I'm not the greatest.*
> *I'm the double greatest!"*
>
> *Muhammad Ali*

The importance of a determined belief system is that it is congruent to the intensity at which you will persist and endure especially when things turn against you. A strong belief system is equal to a strong resolve. If you really truly believe that you can and will do something, it only makes sense that you will not give up until you have attained your goal. You should have as little doubt about achieving your goal as you have any doubt that the sun will rise again tomorrow morning. The vision that you have of your success should be the one and only vision of your future. There are no other options, failure is not an option.

The Spanish explorer Cortez exemplified this mentality in the Spring of 1519 after landing his ships on the Eastern coast of Mexico and experiencing many hardships. He decided to burn his fleet, thus giving himself and his men no other option but to overcome their obstacles. Retreat was not an option because they had no where to run. Failure was not an option; failure would lead to death. Success was the only option. Attack life and this framework with this mentality and you will experience the life style that you deserve and have imagined for yourself.

PAST SUCCESSES

> *"The dictionary is the only place that success comes before work."*
>
> *Vince Lombardi*

So if creating this belief system is so important, how come more people are not able to create a more empowering belief system of their own? In other words, why do some people have the self-efficacy or belief that they can accomplish anything in life, while others are uncertain they can be successful with even the smallest objectives? What it comes down to is the experiences both personal and historical that a person has in place to support their individual belief system. Think of your belief system as a tabletop and various past successes as the support legs for the belief system. The belief system will only be as strong as the legs or experiences that support it.

The Roger Bannister phenomenon is the perfect example of how powerful past successes can be when establishing a belief system. On May 6, 1954 Roger Bannister ran the first ever in recorded history sub 4-minute mile in 3m 59.4s. It was deemed "impossible" by many athletic and physiology experts. There were many doubts that the *human body* was even *capable* of accomplishing this epic feat. Just *46 days later* John Landy also broke the four minute barrier. Then within three years *16 different* runners also broke through the "impossible" four minute barrier. You talk about a strong support leg! The beauty of gathering various past experiences is that they do not have to be your own successes; they can be successes taken from anybody, just as John Landy and 16 other runners had used Bannister's success to support their own belief.

Another point to consider is that not all of the experiences or support legs need to be of the same magnitude and carry the same weight. For example, the current world record holder for men in the 1- mile race is Noureddine Morceli of Algeria who ran the mile in 3m 44.39s in 1993. So any person who desires to run a sub four-minute mile would perhaps use Morceli as the "anchor" experience and Bannister as a supplemental experience. The rational would be that if Morceli can break the barrier by over *15 seconds* and an athlete (Bannister) with an inferior training and diet regimen could do it nearly 50 years ago, then I too, with proper training, can certainly break the four-minute barrier.

So as you create your belief system to accomplish this investing framework, think about what experiences you will use to support it, what experiences will anchor the belief, and what will supplement the belief. What if you knew of somebody that bought 10 houses at the same time? Or what if I told you of a 23-year old that bought three houses at the same time? Would you look at your circumstances differently? Or ask yourself who do you know that has accomplished the framework before? Do you currently make enough income that would allow you to acquire one property a year for 10 years? Do you already have one or more rental properties? Have you ever bought a home before? Do you know somebody that has bought a home before? Starting with small or seemingly insignificant experiences may be all that you have to build on; sometimes this is all you need to begin.

A debilitating factor for many individuals is that their belief system is limited by their personal past experiences. Perhaps you have failed in business before, or you were fired from your job, or you were unsuccessful with a pyramid business opportunity; or even worse, you had a rental property before and you ended up getting rid of it after a year because of the "hassles."

Your past is not your future; don't look back at the past if it will not benefit you. Absolutely rid yourself of your limiting belief systems; you are not the same person you were five years ago, or even five days ago, you have changed, matured, grown; you are wiser, stronger, better. Your past experiences do not make you who you are, but rather *your* vision of *your* future will make you. Don't look back on what you could have or should have done with past opportunities if it is not going to benefit you. Learn and take from these experiences what will benefit you, and forget the rest.

So if years before you owned a rental property and you got rid of it after a year because of the "hassles," learn what caused those obstacles; should you have had more capital reserves; should you have done a better job of screening the tenant, or better yet, should you have hired a professional property manager; or did you acquire the wrong type of property? Analyze what went wrong so that you don't make the same mistake again; get back at it and make it happen.

When you were a kid and you played t-ball or little league, did you quit or retire from the game after you struck out once? Of course not! You probably understood that even the best hitters strike out and that it is just part of the game. And then you discovered that the more you played the more you improved and the less you struck out because you learned from your mistakes and you continued to practice. In fact, the year Mark McGwire broke the single season home run record when he hit 70, he also struck out 155 times; this was equal to the number of games he played in! So the reality is that if you go to the plate enough times you are bound to strike out sooner or later; but by consistently stepping up to the plate, amazing things will happen for you.

SEEING THE BENEFIT

> *"I hated every minute of the training, but I said, don't quit. Suffer now and live the rest of your life as a champion."*
>
> *Muhammad Ali*

It takes a very clear and confident understanding of the end result or payoff of the investing campaign to establish this belief system. Although statistically the framework provides a very profitable return on your time and money invested, there is no "100 percent money-back guarantee" that the actions that you take towards this framework will be able to accomplish your desired outcome. In fact there will *never* be an investment strategy that provides this much wealth accumulation in such a short period of time that will be able to provide a guarantee. Despite this insecurity and instability, this seems to be the only way throughout history in which great feats have been accomplished. Any great accomplishment throughout time was initially almost drowned with skepticism, pessimism, and doubt. However, those who truly believed advanced confidently towards their goal. Sometimes taking a calculated risk is the only thing in life that is worth doing and worth committing yourself to.

Developing a sound belief system is similar to developing your own reality to live in. In essence, what this is saying, is that you create your own perceptions and your own attitudes towards the real world. Although we are all in the same world, it is obvious that there is a dichotomy in how each of us perceives the world to be.

Some people see the world through jaded and cynical eyes while others see the world full of opportunity. Why is this? The majority of us are being exposed to the same media and life experiences; why is it that some individuals quit before they start, and others won't stop until they have reached their goal? The reason: it is their belief system.

The key to establishing focus and a strong belief system is to train your mind to work like a filter. You can retain and forget or erase any information that you are exposed to. Your mind is also able to create any belief system or emotion and accept it as being true or real. The reality of it is that your subconscious can not tell the difference between real experiences and the experiences that you imagine. Because of these absolutely amazing abilities you are able to, in essence, create your own reality. You can believe yourself to be destined for success or failure; it is your choice.

If you are having a tough time buying into this idea, try acting as though you have already experienced success. What are you going to do with your new found time, freedom, and money? Grow it, spend it on houses and cars, start another business? How will you feel, relaxed, energetic? As you begin to act as though you have already experienced success, your actions will lead your mind to believe the new reality you are creating for yourself.

This type of thinking is not any different from how we thought when we were children. We lived in our own worlds, unaffected by others. As we grew older we became more self-conscious, and we let others bring us down to what they believed to be true about us; and in so doing we greatly reduced our ability to think creatively and optimistically.

Use your mind to your advantage; believe yourself to have achieved success, someone that can accomplish massive achievements in real estate. Believe it; then do it.

As you believe and act, you will find everything that you are looking for. In the process of developing your belief system, you will come across many things, people, circumstances, and places that you would have never noticed had you not alerted your subconscious mind to them via your new belief system.

FOCUS ON WHAT YOU WANT

"Some men see things as they are, and say, why? I dream of things that never were, and say, why not?"

George Bernard Shaw

The problem that many people have with their goals and dreams is that they focus their energy, emotions, and attention on what they don't want to happen instead of what they do want to achieve. They are concentrating on what they do not want to have in their lives instead of what they do want to have in their lives.

The unfortunate reality of this circumstance is that you will attract to you what your mind focuses on the most. Although it is on a subconscious level, your current circumstances have been attracted to or drawn to you by the thoughts that you create. So if you focus on not having money or on your struggles, then you will end up broke and frustrated. If you focus on where you are going and the abundance that you will have, then you will get to where you want to go and obtain the wealth you want to have.

Discovering What Was Always There

"That is what learning is. You suddenly understand something you've understood all your life, but in a new way."

Doris Lessing

We need to keep in mind that we are not creating a new you or creating success; we are in fact uncovering the power and the potential that was there all along, within you. As Michelangelo once philosophically explained his magnificent sculptures, he did not create the sculpture but rather he uncovered the beauty that lay within the slab of rock. The same is true for you; you do not have to create a new you. The financial and psychological changes you desire for your life lay within you. All you have to do is chip away at the stone slab and uncover the masterpiece.

By using your mind to see the end result, to "begin with the end in mind" as Stephen Covey would say in his book *The 7 Habits of Highly Effective People*, it is much easier to chip away to uncover your potential; it takes the mystery out of it. You already know what you want the masterpiece to look like; it is only a matter of progressing towards it each and every day. Slowly but consistently you will uncover your own version of Michelangelo's "David" and perhaps you too can slay Goliath, and in your own reality conquer any goal that you have set for yourself no matter how daring or inconceivable it may seem right now.

The bottom line is this; whatever you are looking for, you will find, be sure to look for the right things to feed and create a strong belief system. And so when the student is ready, the teacher will show up.

> *"We sow our thoughts*
> *and we reap our actions.*
> *We sow our actions*
> *and we reap our habits.*
> *We sow our habits*
> *and we reap our character.*
> *We sow our character*
> *and we reap our destiny!"*
>
> *Anonymous*

POINTS TO REMEMBER: CREATE A BELIEF SYSTEM

1.) If you truly believe you can do something, you will take the necessary actions to move forward. If you don't believe you can do something, you won't take action.

2.) It is not unusual for people to lose money, short-term, in real estate investments.

3.) Before you can achieve anything physically, you must accomplish the goal in your mind first.

4.) The importance of a determined belief system is that it is congruent to the intensity at which you will persist and endure especially when things turn against you.

5.) An effective belief system must have a support system. What it comes down to is the experiences both personal and historical that a person has in place to support their individual belief system.

6.) It takes a very clear and confident understanding of the end result or payoff of the investing campaign to establish this belief system.

7.) The problem that many people have with their goals and dreams is that they focus their energy on what they don't want to happen instead of what they do want to achieve.

8.) We need to keep in mind that we are not creating a new you or creating success; we are in fact uncovering the power and the potential that was there all along, within you.

CHAPTER 3
HAVE A VISION

"The empires of the future are the empires of the mind."

Sir Winston Churchill

The overriding purpose of visualizing is to create your future before you get there. Visualizing is perhaps the most empowering way to initiate a massive change in your emotional expectancy. By using visualization, you enable yourself to develop on a subconscious, and most importantly, *emotional* level the reality that you desire. Visualizing leads to success because it provides to your subconscious multiple images and emotions with only one outcome, success. The reality for your subconscious is that it can not comprehend any outcome other than success. Failure is literally not an option; it cannot be imagined.

Imagery or visualization has become a significant component of the training regimen for Olympic and professional athletes. You have probably heard Olympic athletes say as they are getting interviewed after winning their gold medal, "it felt like I had already done it before," or, "it was just like I had envisioned it would be." If you have ever watched the Olympics, you have probably heard these types of testimonials so many times that they seem like a cliché. The reality is that it is not a cliché; these athletes mentally rehearse their success as part of their training regimen. They understand that their outcome is directly linked to their psychology and their ability to experience the desired emotions *before* the actual desired goal comes to pass.

These athletes are aware that to succeed at the highest levels, they need to be more mentally prepared and psychologically stronger than their competitors. There is only so much training that can be done on a physical level before you run into injuries, burnout, or diminishing results. Imagery training allows athletes to get the edge. And so you too should train your mind to rehearse your desired outcome, to experience the emotions you will have when you are financially independent, when you have so much wealth and freedom that you don't know what to do with it.

In fact, even Albert Einstein credits his understanding of the relationship between time and light and the theory of relativity to his ability to use visualization techniques. He asked himself, "What would it be like to ride on a beam of light?" His conclusion was that the faster you travel, the more time slows down. This fact, discovered through the use of visualization, shook the foundation of the scientific community.

Try this mind-body experiment to see first-hand the power of imagery training. Take a string or neck chain approximately 14-16 inches long and put a bolt or a ring through it. Stabilize your elbow on a table and hold both ends of the string or necklace in-between your index finger and thumb with the weight suspended directly below; now using only your mind, your arm is fixed, move the bolt or ring forward and backward, now side to side, and finally clockwise and counterclockwise. Visualize the object moving in the direction that you want it to move in. At first it may be a challenge, but with a little practice you should be able to move the suspended object at your will. What this experiment teaches you is that before you can do something physically, you must rehearse it mentally.

This chapter gives you an opportunity to literally turn off limitations. There are no boundaries to what you can achieve by prudently investing in real estate. Let yourself get excited about the potential you have to create the life you want. Let this potential then drive you to action.

THE BENEFIT IS IN THE DETAILS

> *"Where there is no vision, the people perish."*
>
> *Proverbs, 29:18*

When performing visualization techniques, it is important to account for every detail of your future and the specific experience or experiences. Visualize the freedoms you want for you and your family, your prefect day, the home that you want to finally settle down in, where you want that home to be (remember, real estate is a very mobile investment medium), the cars that you will drive, the other business that you always wanted to start, and the vacations you will take (perhaps to look at property).

Visualize the specific details of the new freedoms you and your family will have. Can you stay at home and spend more time with your kids? Do you want to coach one of their sport teams now that you can commit the time and energy to it? Will you decide to send them to private school for grade school and the Ivy League for their secondary education?

How will your perfect day be scheduled, what time will you wake up now that you don't *have* to work? What new hobbies will you invest your time in? Do you want to learn a martial art, learn to sail, surf, ski, or scuba dive? Maybe you can finally have the time to exercise and eat healthy.

Where do you want to live, in a luxury home, a beach house, or both? Do you want to have two or three vacation homes across the country or the globe in vacation hot spots, places like San Diego, Aspen, Scottsdale, or even New York? What state do you want to live in now that you are not committed to a job?

What cars do you want to drive, the new H-2, a Mercedes-Benz, a Lincoln Navigator, or all three? What colors do you want them to be? Where will you drive them? Maybe it is not a car at all but a boat instead.

Maybe you always wanted to start a business but you never had the money or the time, but now you do. Maybe you want to start a family business so that you can teach your kids the value of hard work and responsibility.

Where and how often do you want to take vacations: Italy, the UK, or Bermuda? Do you want to make an annual tradition of taking your family to a new destination every year?

What would all of these experiences look like, what would they feel like; what do you hear when visualizing the experiences?

Once you can see, feel, taste, hear and smell the details of your future, it will be easy to begin to take the necessary actions to move you forward. It is critical to begin to live your life the way you have visualized it, with the successes you have imagined. If you believe that you will be a millionaire, begin to act like a millionaire, now. Be generous with others; have systems for your money, carry yourself with confidence and charisma. Once you begin to act on the characteristics you want to possess, you will begin to develop them as habits and before you know it, you will be whom you have visualized.

Perhaps one of the most beneficial visualization exercises that you can do is to visualize your eightieth birthday party. Some experts suggest your funeral but I feel the moment should be one of joy and not pain or sorrow. It should be something to look forward to and not be frightened of. Visualize who would be there, how many generations of children are there because of you. How wealthy are you? How is your health, both physical and mental? Have you done everything you said you were going to do? Are you still trying to climb mountains or are you in a valley? Where is the party held? Do you have regrets? Have you left a legacy behind? By asking yourself these questions now, you will be able to create your future to the way that you desire. Be sure to incorporate every finite detail. The more vivid details you include, the more real the vision becomes to your subconscious, and the better results you will experience from the practice.

REHEARSAL

"We are what and where we are because we have first imagined it."

Donald Curtis

Rehearse these programs twice a day, morning and night, so that your subconscious can experience the emotions that you will experience during your successes. Make it a habit or a ritual that you cannot overlook. Just as you would (hopefully) not leave your house without brushing your teeth, you should not leave your house until you have rehearsed. If you don't rehearse your vision, you will not attract the circumstances that you desire.

Find a peaceful room or scenic location where you can be completely undisturbed. Maybe bring a walk-man or disc-man so that you can listen to some of your favorite or most inspiring songs. Relax your body, close your eyes, and visualize the specific scenarios that are important to you. Attempt to visualize each experience without thought interruption. Do not let any other thoughts or stimulus enter your mind.

Like with anything else in life, the more you do something, the better you become at it. We are looking for progress not perfection. This is most certainly the case with visualizing. After performing the technique repeatedly, you will become more proficient with the skill, and you will not be able to imagine any other future for yourself other than the one you have created.

LIVE YOUR VISION

"Vision without action is a daydream. Action without vision is a nightmare."

Japanese Proverb

Once you develop a vision, whatever it may be, it is absolutely essential that you follow through with your intentions. Once you glimpse your vision, you owe it to yourself to bring it fruition. There is no going back; once you know the truth, nothing else will ever bring you peace of mind and satisfaction in your life. There cannot be another alternative in your life other than your awe-inspiring vision. If another alternative even crosses your mind, you must erase it as quickly as it came. The more you dwell on it, the more it will grow. Extinguish the negative or alternative vision as if it were a fire that can destroy your dream home.

Begin living your vision today. The train is not coming in. This means that all of the mind-training that you have performed must now be put into a plan and then into action as soon as possible. You have imagined and visualized your future, now live it. Live as if you are in the future. Live as if you are the person you have imagined.

It is very easy to imagine the future but to live in the present. It is the often heard excuse that "I will stop or start doing "x" when "y" happens." The harsh reality is that "y" is *not* going to happen *until* you stop or start doing "x."

When I worked as a personal trainer in college I would hear *reasons* for not doing what needed to be done all the time. "I'll start eating better once I start seeing some results." Or, "I'll do cardio when I need to lose the last five pounds." Well, of course, you won't see results until you start eating better and doing cardio now! So the same holds true for this investment campaign; you must make the connection from the present to the future now. Do what needs to be done, now.

Do not let your current circumstances or obstacles stand in your way of your vision. Money shortages or credit problems will always be in your life in one shape or another. As long as you have a vision and a plan, all obstacles can be overcome in time.

> *"The best way to predict the future is to invent it."*
>
> *Alan Kay*

POINTS TO REMEMBER: HAVE A VISION

1.) Create your future in your mind first before you create it in reality.

2.) When performing visualization techniques, it is important to account for every detail of your future and the specific experience.

3.) Rehearse this vision morning and night so that your subconscious can experience the *emotions* that you will experience during your successes. By doing this rehearsal, you will begin to attract that which you visualized.

4.) Once you develop a vision, whatever it may be, it is absolutely essential that you follow through with your intentions.

CHAPTER 4 DEVELOP A PLAN

"Men are born to succeed, not fail."

Henry David Thoreau

MODELING

"If I have seen further it is by standing on the shoulders of giants."

Isaac Newton

Studying successful people and their experiences is the most effective means of learning how to accomplish what you want in the shortest amount of time with the least amount obstacles. In fact, modeling people or inventions is the only way that our civilization has ever been able to evolve and prosper throughout time. Every new invention, business idea, medication, scientific theory, philosophy, and even art form has evolved or transformed from one previous to it. Each of these previous historic aspects was a prelude to what we see before us today. If we were to never learn from those before us, we would still be living in the dark ages in caves and hunting wooly mammoths. Thankfully we have evolved.

By this rational, it makes sense that you should do your homework on successful investors and their strategies not only in real estate but also in other financial markets and determine what allowed them to be successful. You should learn from their mistakes and profit from their wisdom. In so doing, you will be following the evolutionary process that has taken place for millions of years.

There have been hundreds of truly amazing individuals throughout history that have achieved absolutely massive amounts of wealth, people like Rockefeller, Getty, Carnegie, Gates, Buffet, and Trump. Put yourself in their shoes and begin to think as they would have thought, act as they would have acted. You will be amazed at how many new perspectives and ideas will be created through this process. This investment in education will generate more powerful returns than any other investment you could ever make.

GOAL SETTING

> *"Make no little plans: they have no magic to stir men's blood and probably them-selves will never be realized. Make big plans."*
>
> *Daniel H. Burnham*

Establishing written goals is the foundation for success in any endeavor in life. Just as you must know where you want to go before you jump in the car and go for a drive so that you don't end up in a bad section of town, you must also know where you want to go with your financial life or investing framework; otherwise you may end up broke, defeated, homeless, or perhaps a combination of all three.

The most amazing of accomplishments are begun first through goal setting. Goal setting is driven by a burning desire to accomplish a specific and measurable objective. It is an objective so bold that it will inspire you to take action. The goal setting should include realistic yet challenging long and short-range outcome goals with specific dates, as well as process goals. Most importantly, the goals need to be written down and reviewed daily.

It is critical that your goal or goals are first and foremost bold. If it doesn't excite you, you will have no desire to act on it and see it through to completion. In addition, nobody else will get excited by it, and you won't be able to get any help with achieving your goal. If you are going to do something, do it big. Would you rather hit a home run during batting practice or hit a home run to win the World Series?

There is a fine line between setting a bold yet realistic goal and one that is bold and unrealistic. In essence, it should be humanly or mathematically possible to achieve your goal. So if your goal is to become a millionaire in 12 months, and you don't have a cardboard box to sleep in or a pot to you-know-what in, you may need to adjust the time frame for accomplishing your ambition, or have one *heck* of a game plan. A more realistic goal for you is to be financially independent in 10 years. This has been done and does continue to be done, with a little bit of work.

The other factor to consider with unrealistic goal setting is that, if you are not successful at accomplishing your objective in the time frame you specified, you could become disappointed or burned out and forget about the goal all together.

Long-range and inspiring outcome goals allow you to generate a big enough "why?" These are the goals that will keep you up late at night and get you up early in the morning. They will give you a sense of purpose with everything you do. Setting these types of goals will not only inspire you but others around you as well. It will motivate others to help you in your game. Your life will never be the same once you make a real commitment to achieve your goal. Your life will truly have more meaning.

It is also important to establish short-range outcome goals that lead up to the objective or primary goal. The smaller goals act as stepping stones for achieving the larger goal. So if you want to buy 10 properties in 10 years, you buy one property now, the first year. As you begin to accomplish the smaller goals, you generate a massive amount of momentum and before you know it you are well on your way. Be careful though, small goals will only motivate to a small extent. They will only change your life in a small way.

With both long and short-range outcome goals, it is important to set a date for the objective. Again, be sure this date is realistic, but it should also be a challenge to meet the deadline. A date allows you to measure time which is the scoreboard for the game.

An outcome goal is one in which you are only concerned about the outcome of an objective; it is more quantitative in nature. This may mean being a millionaire in 10 years or having 10 properties in 10 years. Outcome goals are black and white; either you did or you didn't accomplish the objective. There are two problems with setting just outcome goals exclusively as opposed to outcome and process goals.

First, you do not always have 100 percent control of a situation or an outcome. You may not be able to control keeping your job for the next 10 years or from being surprised by thousands of dollars in medical bills.

The second situation that arises with outcome goals is that once you achieve a specific goal, there is no where else to go but to set a new outcome goal for yourself, one that is even more challenging. Although this may seem like a great thing, you will find that you will never be content. No money will ever be enough if you continually set monetary outcome goals for yourself. You will never be in a state of abundance.

With process goals you have complete control; you control the process of an action. You can control practicing your imagery everyday and writing down and reviewing your goals daily. There are no external forces that can act on these processes for you.

The message to be taken from this is that both outcome and process goals are necessary for success, but the importance that is placed upon each is of the utmost significance. It only makes sense that if something is out of your control, you should not place too much emphasis on it. An example of this would be if you wanted to save $15,000 a year to acquire properties. While this would be nice, maybe comforting, it is not necessary to acquire a property with your own money. So you would not want to make this $15,000 a do or die outcome. If you can train your mind to become more process oriented, you can never be let down by extraneous forces, and the outcome goals will be a natural offspring of this type of process. So instead of saving $15,000 a year and having this be a must for an outcome goal, you could instead make your process goal to put in 12 offers a year for a seller to carry financing or to participate in the Ameridream program. This *is* a process goal; it is something you can control. (This is just an example; this framework does not require these types of acquisition methods)

The understanding is that the process goals that you implement on a daily basis will lay the foundation for accomplishing the short and long-range outcome goals. For example, your process goals are one, review your short and long-range outcome goals daily, and two, visualize the experiences daily. By performing these process exercises, you communicate to your subconscious on an emotional level that you are committed to achieving your outcome goals. The long-range outcome goal is to own 10 properties in 10 years. And the short-range outcome goal is to acquire one property this year.

On a side note, be certain that when setting goals you do not set alternative goals that are secondary to your supreme goal. There is a possibility that you may not accomplish your objective on the first try. Because of this, if you have a fallback plan, the odds are likely that you will fallback and forget about your primary goal. Do not allow this to happen. Don't set alternative goals; you must believe that you will accomplish your primary goal; but it may take more than one try.

WRITE IT DOWN AND REVIEW IT

"First, have a definite, clear, practical ideal-a goal, an objective. Second, have the necessary means to achieve your ends-wisdom, money, materials, and methods. Third, adjust all of your means to that end."

Aristotle

Perhaps the most critical component to not only establishing but also accomplishing your goals is to take pen to paper and not only write them down but review them daily.

In Mark McCormack's book *What They Don't Teach You at Harvard Business School,* he tells of a study that was done on the graduating Harvard MBA class of 1979. Upon graduating, only three percent had written down very clear goals with plans for achieving them. Thirteen percent had goals but they were not in written form nor did they have a specific plan. The remaining 84 percent did not have any goals or direction at all.

Just ten years later, the graduating class was again interviewed. Not surprisingly, the three percent minority that had specific written goals were earning on average *ten times* as much as their other classmates *combined!* Clearly there is massive power in writing down your goals with specific plans to achieve them.

Reviewing your goals daily is also a critical component to achieving your objective. Just as you visualize your outcomes morning and night, you must also review your specific goals morning and night. Keep an itemized and updated list of all of your goals with you at all times. Perhaps store them in your day planner or your briefcase so that they will always be a part of your every day.

Evaluate what actions you took during the day that brought you closer to the goal, and what actions need to be taken tomorrow to continue to move you forward. Remember, even the longest journeys, and the most daunting of goals, begin with a single step forward.

> *"Small opportunities are often the beginning of great enterprises."*
>
> *Demosthenes*

SYSTEMS

> *"A task begun is half done."*
>
> *Horace, Epistulae 2.40*

Gordon Bethune the CEO of Continental Airlines talks about systems in his book, *From Worst to First – Behind the Scenes of Continental's Remarkable Comeback.* His theory is that what gets measured gets managed. I tend to agree and that is why this part of the chapter is so critical to your success. If you are not tracking or measuring something, it is impossible for you to focus on it and improve it. Bethune measured variables like the percentage of bags lost, the percentage of on-time flights, and the number of sick days taken by employees. By tracking these types of variables and putting systems in place to improve them, he was able to turn Continental Airlines from a doomed company to a perennial powerhouse in the airline industry.

This same strategy of systems can work wonders for you as well as your beginning to move forward with acquiring properties and building a real estate business. In Chapter 7, Learn the Business, we will focus on the monetary systems like P&L and cash flow statements and projections that will be implemented for you to successfully run your business; but for now we will focus on the day to day and psychological systems that you can begin using now. These systems include a prioritized "to do" list, a contact sheet, an itemized objective plan, an itemized life plan, and a productivity constant.

First, I owe thanks to Stephen Covey for his contribution of his prioritized "to do" list from his book *The 7 Habits of Highly Effective People*. Basically there are four quadrants, Important Urgent, Not Important Urgent, Important Not Urgent, and Not Important Not Urgent. Each objective that you have will be accordingly placed under each quadrant. What this allows you to do are two things; first you write down *everything* you need to do in the near future, and second, you can prioritize in what order these items needs to be accomplished. A good objective is to accomplish at least one item on your list everyday. This strategy will keep you moving forward and in continual motion. On the next page is a sample of what this system looks like.

To Do List

Important Urgent	Not Important Urgent
Important Not Urgent	**Not Important Not Urgent**

The second system is the contact sheet. This allows you to track the contacts that you make in chronological order. You can see with whom you spoke to, when you spoke to them, how you spoke to them (e-mail/person/phone), what you spoke to them about, and whether or not you need to speak to them again. Literally every phone call that comes in about a rental that is available or from a business associate will be documented. You won't have to worry about forgetting names, phone numbers, or conversations. You will however want to format the columns for this system. The spreadsheet below has been minimized so it will fit on this page.

Contact Sheet

Date	Time	Contact Person	Phone #	Topic Of Disc.	C/B

The itemized objective plan that you will use is specifically designed for this 10-year framework. This plan will include the people, places, and things you will need in order for you to be successful. In other words, you will have a date set for every objective that needs to be met for acquiring 10 properties in 10 years. This list will include establishing relations with a Real Estate Planner®, a lender, an accountant, an insurance agent, and probably a property management company just to name a few of the people that will help you along the way. Other objectives that will need to be met will include having your credit pulled to see where you stand, and perhaps opening a cash management account for the down-payment on your 1st property.

The itemized life plan has a much broader and inspiring scope for your goals. Your life plan will include all of the possibilities *after* you have accomplished the 10-year framework: objectives like opening another business, where you want to live, what type of home you want to own, and what type of car you want to drive.

The Productivity Constant is the measure of how effective you have been on a daily basis. It measures the process goals for this framework and your life. It is a physical chart that allows you to evaluate day in and day out, if were you able to bring yourself one step closer to accomplishing your ultimate goal or dream. The productivity constant is a way to keep score. You are either winning the game or losing the game. The understanding is that what you focus on, you bring to you. What you measure, what you manage, is what you accomplish.

The vision of the Productivity Constant originated from my reading of Benjamin Franklin's Auto-Biography. Franklin decided to quantify and measure specific virtues so that he could track his progress or evolution as a man and attempt to live, in his eyes, the perfect day. He decided on thirteen virtues that were more important to success than others, these included, temperance, silence, order, resolution, frugality, industry, sincerity, justice, moderation, cleanliness, tranquility, chastity, humility – and to imitate Jesus and Socrates.

I decided to keep intact Franklin's general idea but to adjust his virtue objectives so as to more acutely meet my own specific process goals. The shift from being value driven to process driven, allowed the results to be much more outcome specific.

I designed a spreadsheet for each month that included the specific daily processes running horizontally across the page and the days of the month running vertically down the left-hand side of the page. I allocated certain columns or time to writing this book, exercising or training, eating healthy, making bold actions or decisions, paying it forward, education, accomplishing objectives on my "to do" list, and several others. As I accomplished a certain process on a specific day I would highlight the day and objective, and then at the end of the month I would calculate the progress so as to compare the processes month to month.

The most significant aspect of this productivity chart was the column labeled, "being bold." I found that the more of these bold actions that I took, the more I accomplished, the more I grew, and the quicker I moved towards my goals. These bold actions would include putting together a mastermind group or team or acquiring a new property. On the following page is a modified template of the Productivity Constant. The column heads have been left blank because of the size limit of the page.

Productivity Constant

Date														
1														
2														
3														
4														
5														
6														
7														
8														
9														
10														
11														
12														
13														
14														
15														
16														
17														
18														
19														
20														
21														
22														
23														
24														
25														
26														
27														
28														
29														
30														
31														
Total %														
High %														

Understandably, you must find the system that will work for you, one that will measure your progress and hold you accountable. But you have to set it up so that you can win at the game; make the goals achievable. This system may or may not work for you, but it is critical that you track your habits, the standards that you have set for yourself.

By doing this you will provide yourself with intrinsic competition. You will not be competing with anybody else but yourself. You will become a more effective and productive person this month than the last month. This chart is the secret to doing and accomplishing everything you want in life. It is the only thing in your life that will hold you accountable for the things you do on a daily basis.

A Sense Of Urgency

"Dream as if you'll live forever. Live as if you'll die today."

James Dean

Navigating through the process of goal setting should drive you in the direction of developing a sense of urgency to take action. It is great to set goals, but if you are not motivated or driven to take action and achieve them, all of the goal setting in the world won't do you any good.

A compelling method that can be used to develop a sense of urgency is to establish and write down dates that require discipline to be achieved. In other words, if you know you can do a project in a month, set the date for 20 days instead. This way you can expedite your goals.

If this example does not seem like a significant improvement or change, it is because it is on such a small scale. At this scale it is a reduction of only 10 days. However, these days add up very quickly over a life time. The reality is that it is a reduction of time by 33 percent.

What if you were to accomplish all of your goals in life 33 percent quicker than you thought possible? So instead of being a millionaire in 15 years, you were to earn that status in 10 years? This is the power of having a sense of urgency in *everything* that you do. The clock is ticking.

POINTS TO REMEMBER: DEVELOP A PLAN

1.) Studying successful people and their experiences is the most effective means of learning how to accomplish what you want in the shortest amount of time with the least amount obstacles.

2.) Establishing written goals is the foundation for success in any endeavor in life. The goal setting should include realistic yet challenging long and short-range outcome goals with specific dates, as well as process goals.

3.) Perhaps the most critical component to not only establishing but also accomplishing your goals is to take pen to paper and not only write them down but review them daily.

4.) If you are not tracking or measuring something it is impossible for you to focus on it and improve it. What gets measured gets managed.

5.) Going through the process of goal setting must drive you in the direction of developing a sense of urgency to take action.

PART TWO

THE PLAN

BUILDING YOUR EMPIRE

CHAPTER 5
BUY AND HOLD

"Be not afraid of growing slowly; be afraid only of standing still."

Chinese Proverb

An investment strategy unexamined is not worth executing. As you navigate through this chapter, carefully examine the framework that is being laid out for you. You will be convinced that this is the most powerful investment initiative that can be implemented by *everybody*.

This chapter identifies the part of the cycle where a home becomes a house, a property, or a unit. The significance in name change is that you can't have any emotional attachment to the property other than to create wealth with it. Regardless of whether you ever lived in the property and what memories you may have, it is now a part of your business. Remember, this is a business that you are starting.

This chapter literally is the next chapter in your investment framework. It will be beneficial for you to read and reread this chapter more than a couple of times and to use it as a resource when questions may arise in the future. This is where things get very exciting in a very short amount of time. This chapter is a quantum leap as far as investment strategies go.

The majority of individuals live their lives without a plan and because of this failure to plan, they plan to fail. The same is true of real estate investors or dabblers. The majority of the horrific real estate stories you hear are from amateurs, people who tried this or tried that and once they hit some tough times or lost money, they were out, period. They did not have a vision or a plan to keep them on track and to keep them committed to a goal. This is the loser's mentality. If you own this thought process, you need to change it before you commit to this framework. When you start investing in real estate you have moved into the major leagues. You are no longer a passive equity investor or trader. You own property. This property has enormous potential but it carries with it an equal amount of risk if there is not a plan in place and if that plan is not managed.

Real Estate investment frameworks and management strategies can be as complicated or as simple as you want them to be. For our purposes we are going to keep it simple. Specifically, the investing campaign or framework has four parts: the acquisition, the holding period, the exchange or sale, and then the replacement.

THE FRAMEWORK

> *"Fortune favors the brave."*
>
> *Phormio Terence*

1.) Specifically the framework is to acquire one new property a year for 10 years.

2.) Hold and rent each one of these properties for a period of 10 years.

3.) At the end of the 10-year holding period for each property, you then sell or preferably exchange the property via a 1031 exchange.

4.) Once the property is sold you acquire one new property. You can then refinance the new property and take your equity or gain out *tax free*. This is the money you can live off of for the current year until the process is repeated the next year.

Although this may seem like an aggressive and daunting framework, keep in mind that the acquisition of the first rental property is always the most psychologically challenging. Things are always difficult before they are easy.

This is the most simplistic and conservative framework. There are other variants that allow for more growth, these will be discussed a little later in this chapter; for now we will keep it simple.

THE ACQUISITION

The critical component of this initiative is to identify the types of properties that will perform well for this campaign. These properties should be newer, in the median to lower price range, perhaps $150,000, have at least three bedrooms, two baths, a two-car garage, and be between 1200 -1700 square feet. These same properties *must not* have pools or spas. We will also take a brief look at the timing of the acquisition as well as how to finance it.

Newer properties are important for three reasons. First, generally speaking, newer neighborhoods will appreciate at a quicker rate than older neighborhoods. Second, ideally, if the house is well-built, you will experience less maintenance expenses on a newer property than you will on older properties. And third, where do most people or tenants want to live? Most people or tenants want to live in a new, clean, and safe house. These are all indicators of a new neighborhood. The golden rule is, if you don't want to live in the house or neighborhood, nobody else will either. Be smart; drive through the neighborhood at different times of day, a gated community is preferable, something close to schools and freeways. Do your homework. These three factors will lend themselves to a healthier bottom-line for you.

The significance of the size and the value or price of the property is two-fold. First, remember you want to appeal to the largest possible market of potential renters. Clearly, this market will be the type of people that live in a 1200-1700 square foot, three bedroom, two bath, two-car garage house. Most of the population does not live in 2000 plus square foot houses. Second, and we will discuss this in more detail later, the CAP rate on a property valued at more than $150,000 begins to spiral steadily downward. In essence, this means you are not generating nearly as much cash flow per dollar invested as you should be receiving if you were to have bought a less expensive property.

Remember, the property is not intended for your use, but rather for a tenant to live in. Pools and spas are a liability, you could be one child drowning or slipping on the cool deck away from a lawsuit. In addition, pools also require more maintenance and provide tenants with another asset to destroy. The reality is that nobody is going to care as much about the condition of your property as you are; the fewer things that can go wrong or be destroyed the better.

The timing of the acquisition is almost a mute point. You can't or shouldn't try to time the market based on rates or hot buyer's markets. If you are waiting for a correction, you are going to be waiting a long time. Very rarely will real estate property values decrease. And if they do, the ability to speculate as to where the bottom of the market is; and when it is going to hit, is impossible. The only historical trend for a temporary down market for real estate *activity* is during the holiday season of November and December. This decrease in activity does not have much of an influence on price, but it may have a stronger influence on whether or not you can rent out your property. It may behoove you to time your purchase and rental agreements not to close or expire during this time period. This being said, there has *never* been a *bad* time to buy real estate, there have just been *better* times.

The key is to maximize your leverage on the investment so that you put down as little money as possible while still being able to pay for the mortgage, taxes, insurance, repairs, and vacancies. Ideally, the property is leveraged so that the rent coming in is equal to or greater than your expenses. Negative cash flow situations are not always a terrible circumstance, but these need to be evaluated on situation specific data. A financial structure that is producing negative cash flow *may* limit the number of properties you would be able to acquire in that manner. For example, having one property that is generating $100 negative cash flow may not put you in a van down by the river, but having four or five of them may very well. The goal during the wealth building stage is not to generate massive cash flow on a single property, but rather to massively leverage the property so as to maximize your return on equity and to reduce your potential tax obligation.

Now that you understand the right and wrong properties to acquire we can take the next step into the investing campaign.

THE HOLDING PERIOD

During the 10-year holding period two very important things are taking place. First the longer you hold onto a property, the more the property will appreciate and you will be able to grow your equity tax free. And second, your payments stay relatively uniform, while at the same time your rental income increases. This concept creates more passive cash flow for you, but it also increases your potential tax base. This unfortunately will begin to present a problem for the years moving forward. And this is part of the reason we only hold a property for 10 years maximum during the wealth building stage.

THE EXCHANGE

The third stage, the exchange. After 10 years of holding a property, you sell or exchange that property. At this point in time, you have a more substantial equity position and less leverage which means your return on equity has become borderline insignificant. You are also producing more and more cash flow from your properties, thus *increasing* your potential tax obligation. *You are off track.* You now sell or preferably exchange the property and "realize" your gain in step four, the replacement stage.

THE REPLACEMENT

The replacement stage allows you to perform a 1031 tax deferred exchange and roll your gain "tax free" into a new property and then refinance and get your gain out, tax free. This refinance allows you to get the majority of your equity out tax free and to again be in a maximum leverage position on the new property. This procedure will minimize the passive cash flow that you were beginning to experience from the original property and at the same time will reduce your potential tax obligation while maximizing your return on equity.

RESULTS

For the sake of simplicity we will take a look at each component of this framework so that the benefits will be clearly defined. The benefits include leveraged-appreciation, cash flow, depreciation, and principal reduction.

First, leveraged-appreciation or leveraged-compounding is the driving force behind this strategy, not just the simple compounding, which many investment advisors call the 8th wonder of the world, but rather leveraged-compounding. Let's take a look at how simple-compounding compares to leveraged-compounding. Simple-compounding is a dollar for dollar investment, much like you would experience in the equities market. Leveraged-compounding is a 10 cents on the dollar investment, much like you would experience in real estate investments. We will assume two things, first, that the investment appreciates at six percent a year and thus the property value will double every 12 years (The Rule of 72); and second that we can in fact acquire a property for 10 cents on the dollar. Both of these assumptions can be validated with data throughout this book.

	Simple-Comp.	Leveraged-Comp.
Today	$1	$10
Year 12	$2	$20
Year 24	$4	$40
Year 36	$8	$80
Year 48	$16	$160
Year 60	$32	$320

With leveraged-compounding you will experience 10 times the rate of return as compared to simple-compounding! Clearly there is no comparison between simple-compounding and leveraged-compounding. So when you see "financial experts" in the newspaper or on TV comparing the rates of appreciation of the equities market versus the real estate market, pay attention to whether or not they are considering the leverage factor.

Now looking at a specific example, a property worth $150,000 today, at six percent appreciation (The median appreciation nationwide has been 6.7 percent over the past 20 years. The average appreciation nationwide has been over 8 percent over the past 20 years. Source: Office of Federal Housing Enterprise Oversight) will be worth $268,627 in 10 years. This investment alone would produce over $118,000 in equity build-up during a 10-year period. This equity is your pay off for the 10th year, until the next year when you refinance your next property and achieve the same results. The $118,000 of growth would equate to a return on the asset of over 79 percent for the 10 years, not including principal reduction or tax savings.

Now we will examine this same example, but this time we will look at the returns based on the leverage factor. Let us assume that we can acquire the property with a 10 percent down conventional loan. This is being conservative because as we will learn there are ways to acquire this same property with three percent down or even nothing down. However, we will use a 10 percent down payment in this example so that we can see a very conservative return on our investment.

Again we will look at this same example of a property valued at $150,000. By using a 10 percent acquisition strategy via a conventional loan, your initial financial exposure will be $15,000. Again, based on the previous example, the same $150,000 property would be worth $268,627 in 10 years. The gain again would be $118,627, not including any principal reduction or tax savings. The return on investment would be $118,627/$15,000 or 791 percent over 10 years. The leveraged return is clearly a much more impressive return than the non-leveraged return in the previous example.

The second factor is passive cash flow; this factor can act as a double-edged sword. For many novice investors, an increase in passive cash flow indicates a step closer to financial independence, the misunderstanding being that if you can increase your passive cash flow to a point that is beyond your expenses, you are considered to be financially independent. While there is some truth to this, this same increase in passive cash flow also presents an increase in your tax base. In addition, this flawed concept also assumes that you are content with your current life style. In essence, you may have enough passive cash flow to pay your bills, but you may still not have the luxuries you desire. Fortunately, this framework does not depend on passive *taxable* cash flow as a measuring stick, but instead it measures success by annual *tax free* capital gains.

For argument sake let us take a look at how the cash flow will proliferate the longer you hold on to a property. Again taking a conservative approach to forecasting the rental increases, we will assume two factors: first that the rental income will increase at a rate of three percent a year, and second, that the property breaks even the first year; in other words, the income is equal to the expenses during the first year.

A $150,000 property could conservatively rent for $1000 a month. The same property in 10 years based on a three percent increase in rent per year would rent for $1344 a month. All taxes and insurance being equal, this property would produce over $300 a month or $3,600 a year positive cash flow.

Depreciation is the third factor; it provides the opportunity to massively decrease your potential tax obligation. Depreciation is based on the concept of wear and tear of commercial equipment, machinery, or in this case investment property. Depreciation allows you to depreciate the structure, not the land, over 27.5 years for a residential investment property and 39 years for a commercial property. For a $150,000 residential investment property it would equate to a potential tax write-off of $3,500 to $4,500 annually.

Fourth, principal reduction is perhaps the least significant benefit that we will examine. While clearly there are benefits of having the tenant pay down your mortgage, the lion's share of the equity buildup will come from the appreciation of the property. For example let's take a look at the 10-year investing life of a $150,000 property. In 10 years the property at six percent appreciation a year will be worth over $268,000. This means that you will have built up over $118,000 in equity based solely on the appreciation of the property. Over these same 10 years, with a loan of 6.5 percent for 30 years, your tenant will have paid $19,763 in principal on the loan; not bad. However, considering the principal reduction equates to just over 14 percent of the overall equity buildup, it is not a factor to start doing cartwheels over. What does all of this mean? A couple of things; first, principal reduction is not tremendously significant, and second, interest only loans, which we will discuss in upcoming chapters, are more powerful than they appear to be.

These four factors equate to financial independence. You can make it difficult and manage the properties yourself, or make it easy and hire somebody to do it. But if you stick to the plan for 10 years, *you will* be financially independent, it is your choice.

The reality of investing in real estate is that it is not sexy; it does provide headaches from tenants complaining about toilets, and yes, you may even lose money some months. But it has worked before in the past, it does work now, and it will continue to work into the future. History tells us this; real estate has had a strong propensity to increase in value, and it will continue to rise in value because it is driven by inflation and by demand.

Detailed below is a forecast for this framework 10 years from today for a single property. It describes the property in terms of value, equity position, cash flow, and annual depreciation. The projections are based on six percent appreciation per year along with a three percent increase in rental income per annum. It is assumed that the property was acquired for $150,000 with a 10 percent down payment and an interest rate of 6.5 percent. The initial rental income was breaking even at $1,000 a month and we are depreciating 75 percent of the structure over 27.5 years. These are all par statistics; there is nothing super-natural about this scenario.

Value	Equity	Cash Flow	Depreciation
$268,627	$153,390	$344 / Month	$4,091

Theoretically, upon refinancing the property in the 10th year, and leaving a 10 percent equity position in the property, you can extract over $120,000, *tax free*, to live off of for that year. And of course the next year the same trend would follow. In fact for the next nine years the same trend will follow. What you decide to do with that equity is up to you. There are additional strategies that can be implemented that will be discussed in further chapters.

So now that we know the benefits, what is the most prudent path to follow to effectively accomplish our goal of 10 property acquisitions in 10 years?

STRAIGHT-LINE ACQUISITION MODEL

The most effective and efficient way to work this investing campaign is to turn your primary residence into a rental. What this allows you to do is to take advantage of terms when you move into your new primary residence. After you have turned your house into a rental, you are able to get into the new property for as little as nothing down, or maybe five percent worst-case scenario; you also obtain a more favorable interest rate. You would not be able to take advantage of either the minimal down payment or favorable interest rate if you were acquiring an investment property as opposed to a primary residence. On the next page is a diagram of how the Straight Line Acquisition Model will work.

Year - 10	=	Rental Property #10
^		
Year - 9	=	Rental Property #9
^		
Year - 8	=	Rental Property #8
^		
Year - 7	=	Rental Property #7
^		
Year - 6	=	Rental Property #6
^		
Year - 5	=	Rental Property #5
^		
Year - 4	=	Rental Property #4
^		
Year - 3	=	Rental Property #3
^		
Year - 2	=	Rental Property #2
^		
Year - 1	=	Rental Property #1
^		
PR		

PR = Primary Residence
The primary residence changes every year during the 10 year Straight-line Acquisition Model.

INSIDE THE BOX ACQUISITION MODEL

> *"There is no security on this earth, there is only opportunity."*
>
> *General MacArthur*

The Inside the Box Acquisition Model has two alternatives. The first is much more conventional but it is also practical for individuals or families that want a stable home and don't want to move every year or two. The second alternative allows for not only the acquisition of rental properties, but it also allows the investor to take advantage of Internal Revenue Code 121.

IRC 121 is a code that pertains to tax free capital gain for property owners. This code is a product of the Taxpayer Relief Act of 1997. It allows for a tax free capital gain or exclusion of up to $500,000 for joint filers and $250,000 for single filers that have lived in and owned their primary residence for two of the past five years. This exclusion is available once every two years.

What both of these alternatives have in common is that they are not quite as friendly or beneficial for the investor in regards to financing terms on the rental properties. By acquiring the property as an investor instead of an owner occupant, the interest rate will be higher and you will be required to put down at least five percent, realistically more likely 10 percent down.

The first alternative allows you and your family to remain in your home for as long as you like. There is no obligation to move. The one caveat being that it will be necessary to refinance your home every two to four years so that you can put your equity to highest and best use and use it to fund the acquisition of other rental properties. This access to equity will support the framework of acquiring one property a year for 10 years. The understanding is to keep your equity working for you and to not only obtain the highest return possible but to also reduce your potential tax obligation via interest write-offs. The longer your equity sits in a property, the less of a return you will get on your equity and the smaller your tax-write-offs will be.

The second alternative is similar to the first in respect to the acquisition of the rental properties, but it varies in that you will move every two years so you can take advantage of IRC 121. Basically, your primary residence would be a platform from which you can expedite the build-up or creation of equity over a two-year period. The most effective ways to do this are to either acquire your primary residence wholesale, build your home yourself, or invest in a primary residence in a new subdivision. After two years you should have built up enough equity to pay for commissions and other cost of sale fees and still be able to roll a significant amount of equity *tax free* into your new primary residence.

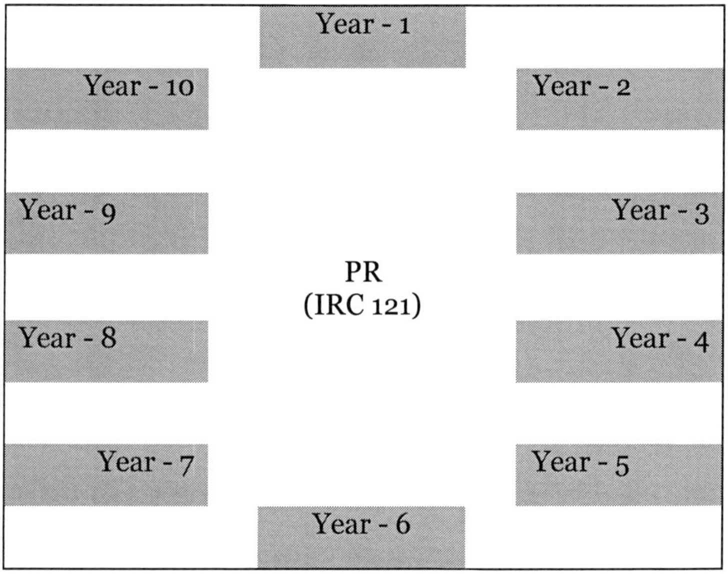

PR = Primary Residence
The primary residence can remain constant during the 10 year Inside the Box Acquisition Strategy or you can take advantage of IRC 121.

The new primary residence, for the sake of this framework, can be of the same or greater value depending upon your debt to income ratios and your goals. If your debt to income ratio is stretched thin, it will be difficult to roll into a significantly larger asset with each move because the only factor you have to offset your debt to income ratio is your ability to invest more equity for a down-payment. So instead of investing just five percent or putting $5,000 down, you may be able to invest 20 percent or put $20,000 down so as to keep your monthly payments consistent. A general rule of thumb is that for every thousand dollars you invest as a down-payment, you reduce your payment by about seven dollars.

If your goal is to own your primary residence free and clear in 10 years, it may behoove you to not move into a larger asset or home every two years. By staying in the same price range of home with every move, you are able to create a stronger equity position every time you move. However, keep in mind this larger down-payment or stronger equity position goes against the rules of maximizing your return on equity and reducing your potential tax obligation.

Here is an example of how moving into a house of equal value every two years will eventually lead to owing your home free and clear. In this example you will own property #1 for years one and two, and property #2 for years three and four, and so on.

SAME VALUE IRC 121 ACQUISITION

Property	Initial Inv.	Value	Appr.	Value In 2 Years	Net After Sale
#1	$0	$250,000	15%	$330,625	$60,787
#2	$60,787	$250,000	15%	$330,625	$121,574
#3	$121,574	$250,000	15%	$330,625	$182,361
#4	$182,361	$250,000	15%	$330,625	$243,148
#5	$243,148	$250,000	15%	$330,625	$303,935

If your debt to income ratio is not stretched too thin and you want to move up in property values so as to live in a more luxurious home and maximize your return on equity and reduce your potential tax obligation, you can continue to leverage yourself with every move and quickly snowball your equity into an enormous property. Another benefit of acquiring larger properties is that every time you move, it allows you to generate more significant amounts or volumes of appreciation. The following is an example of how this strategy of moving up in property value would benefit you.

INCREASE IN VALUE
IRC 121 ACQUISITION

Property	Initial Inv.	Value	Appr.	Value In 2 Years	Net After Sale
#1	$0	$250,000	15%	$330,625	$60,787
#2	$60,787	$300,000	15%	$396,750	$133,732
#3	$133,732	$350,000	15%	$462,875	$218,834
#4	$218,834	$400,000	15%	$529,000	$316,094
#5	$316,094	$450,000	15%	$595,125	$425,511

It is assumed with both of these examples that the property will appreciate at 15 percent annually and that the cost of sale will not exceed six percent. The cost of sale can be minimized by entering into a four percent listing agreement with a Realtor® as opposed to a full six percent. The reality is that Realtors® or Real Estate Planners® like to sell homes. If you agree to have them represent you on your next new home purchase, they will more often than not take a four percent commission to list and sell your current home. The additional two percent cost of sale includes your closing costs and/or escrow fees.

A home is what you make it, a place to live or a foundation for financial independence. This framework may seem a bit daunting but remember, take one step at a time, your risk tolerance will adjust as you begin to take action, and these once daunting strategies will begin to look like wonderful tools that you can use to not only save you money in taxes, but to also create a fortune along the way.

WHAT ARE THE MASSES DOING?

> *"Two roads diverged in a wood, and I – I took the one less traveled by, and that has made all the difference."*
>
> *Robert Frost*

The wise consensus is that you should research and observe what most people are doing, and do the opposite, your chances are far better. Statistically, the majority of people are not financially independent and they do not have an abundance of wealth. This point has been made painfully obvious by the increasing amount of bankruptcies and credit card debt that is being stockpiled by Americans. Because of this, it clearly makes sense to do something, anything, financially different from what the masses are doing.

So what are the masses doing? The masses are doing one of two things when it comes to real estate and home ownership. They are either being very secure and conservative with their real estate decisions, or they are being very aggressive, both of which are deadly when it comes to this framework. The minority of people out there fit into the third genre, the real estate investor. These three types can be characterized by three points. How long they have lived in their house, what their equity position is in that house, and what the expense (mortgage) to gross income ratio is. We will take a look at the profile of all three types of these homeowners.

THE CONSERVATIVE HOME OWNER

The conservative or secure homeowner is characterized by having historically lived in a home for at least 10 years, they move out of necessity, usually to relocate out of state or to add a bedroom for a growing family, but never for the sake of buying a more luxurious home. They have a very strong equity position and their mortgage and other expenses are less than 38 percent of their gross income. They use their excess take home income to eat out, go on vacations, or save for retirement through an IRA or a 401K. Their ultimate goal is to get their home paid for so they can own it free and clear; they try to accomplish this by having their mortgage on a 15-year as opposed to a 30-year note.

THE AGGRESSIVE HOME OWNER

The aggressive homeowner is just the opposite of the conservative homeowner. The aggressive home owner moves frequently, perhaps every two to five years. Their objective for moving is to move *up* in home value. When they can afford it, and often times when they can't, they will move into a nicer neighborhood or a more luxurious home; very rarely will the move be made out of necessity. They acquire the largest home that they can get a loan for. This means a highly leveraged property, and a debt to income ratio well above 38 percent. They are pushing the red line. These individuals are house poor or broke. Their homes are scarcely furnished, and every month it is a stretch for them to make their mortgage payment. They will usually not have enough disposable income for vacations, eating out, or material purchases; they will fund these purchases through credit cards. Retirement planning or establishing a savings is not even an afterthought for them. The aggressive homeowner also has no desire to pay off their home; they will always use a 30-year note to pay for their property.

THE INVESTOR HOME OWNER

This breed, hopefully you included, is the prudent combination of the conservative and aggressive home owner. The investor does move frequently, ideally at the minimum of once every two years if they are in the wealth accumulation stage. They move for one of two reasons, either to turn their property into a rental, or to take advantage of IRC 121. These IRC 121 moves allow them to maximize their return on investment and their tax write-off opportunities. Their debt ratio does not exceed 38 percent of their monthly gross income so they are still able to save money to use for their next property acquisition in the upcoming year. The investor is also savvier and will use interest-only loans to support the acquisition of rental properties and to maximize their return on equity and to reduce their potential tax obligation. Depending on what investment stage they are in, investors will use either a 30 or 15-year note to meet their overall objective. These investors understand delayed gratification and are willing to put off the harvest of their work for at least 10 years. They understand that in 10 years they will be financially independent.

Vacation Homes & Land

So we know we are going to be an investor, and that we are going to follow the Straight Line Acquisition Model or the Inside the Box Acquisition Model. What about investing in land or vacation homes? Don't, at least not during the wealth building stages. The one thing both the Straight-Line Acquisition Model and the Inside the Box Acquisition Model have in common is that other people, tenants, are "buying" your assets or paying for your mortgages. This is an important point. You in essence leverage the acquisition not only financially but also through the work and payments of your tenant. You would not or should not do it without them. Quite often investors overlook this factor when they acquire 2nd or 3rd homes or even land.

These "assets" which are really more like liabilities if *you* are making the payment, are not a prudent acquisition if you are trying to build a self-sustaining wealth creating system, like the one that is detailed in this book.

Vacation homes are great for vacations, not necessarily for investments. First, the likelihood of your being able to vacation there when *you* want to and still be able to rent it out and have your debt service covered by a tenant is very unlikely. Second, even if the debt service can be accomplished, you may not enjoy returning to your vacation home to find things stolen, not working, damaged, or dirty. If you are going to move forward with the idea, keep a vacation home just that, a vacation home, not a rental property.

Vacant land has two potentials, one is in harmony with this framework, one is not. First, acquiring land to *immediately* build a property on can be a very powerful way to minimize "acquisition costs." Often times you can build a property for less money than you can buy one from a builder. This is a great way to take the first step to taking advantage of IRC 121.

Second, acquiring land and sitting on it *may* be a good *long-term* investment *if* you have the cash flow to support it. But it is not a self-sustaining investment, and it is often very speculative in nature. Quite often, land is bought in the hopes that in 5 or 10 years it will become more valuable due to urban sprawl. Unfortunately, climates and trends change and there is the opportunity for those 5 or 10 years to turn into 15 or 20 years. If you want to gamble, then land speculation is a good idea. If you want a sure thing, stick to the framework in this book.

Hopefully, by now, you should begin to understand that the information you are being provided with is an amazing opportunity. Seize it and act on it; learn from those that have traveled the path before you.

> *"To know the road ahead, ask those coming back."*
>
> *Chinese Proverb*

POINTS TO REMEMBER: BUY & HOLD

1.) This chapter identifies the part of the cycle where a home becomes a house, a property, or a unit.

2.) When you start investing in real estate you have moved into the major leagues. You own property that has enormous potential but also an equal amount of risk if it is not managed.

3.) The framework is to acquire one new property a year for 10 years. Rent each one of these properties for 10 years. At the end of the 10 year holding period, sell the property. As you sell the property you replace it with a new property via a 1031 exchange. Once into the new property, refinance the unit and take your equity or gain out TAX FREE. This is the money you can live off of for the next year until the process is repeated. Or you can reinvest the whole sum into multiple properties.

4.) The properties must be newer, in the price range of $150,000, have at least three bedrooms, two baths, and a two car garage, and be between 1200 -1700 square feet. These same houses must not have pools or spas.

5.) The Straight-Line Acquisition Model is the most effective and efficient way to work this investing campaign. It allows you to turn your primary residence into a rental. What this allows you to do is to take advantage of terms when you move into your next property.

6.) Inside the Box Acquisition Model is a much more conventional approach but perhaps not quite as friendly or beneficial for the investor in regards to financing terms. In essence this strategy allows you to stay put in your home and not have to move while still being able to acquire one property a year for ten years with investor financing or you can take advantage of IRC 121.

7.) The returns are amazing! If the $150,000 rental property appreciates at just six percent for 10 years or to over $268,000, including principal reduction, you will have over $135,000 in equity in ten years.

8.) Vacation homes and land are not "assets" but are more like liabilities if *you* are making the payment. They are not a prudent acquisition if you are trying to build a self-sustaining wealth creating system, like the one that is detailed in this book.

CHAPTER 6 ACQUISITION STRATEGIES

"Knowledge is power."

Sir Francis Bacon

If you have read this far, you should understand that you acquire properties for two reasons and two reasons only, to maximize your return on equity and to reduce your potential tax obligation. Both of these variables go hand in hand with a highly leveraged property.

This chapter will discuss financial literacy for real estate investments. In particular it will identify and explain four important factors, acquisition strategies, the markets, holding strategies, and the interest rates.

First we will take a look at some avenues that allow you to meet the acquisition objectives. These avenues include lease purchases and land trusts. We will identify more traditional financing techniques using other people's money in Chapter 11.

Second, these acquisition techniques allow you to purchase or acquire properties in the primary, secondary, and tertiary housing markets. These markets represent respectively, first, MLS (Multiple Listing Service) listed properties, second, FSBO's (For Sale By Owner's) or distressed properties, and third, foreclosures and REO (Bank/Lender owned) properties.

Third, there is clearly a safe way to legally hold property, and there is a reckless way. This chapter will provide you with some of the pros and cons to certain structures.

Fourth, we will take an economic approach and examine how interest rates affect housing prices and property values.

LEASE PURCHASE

Lease Purchases or rent-to-owns are very similar to that of a seller carry back (Chapter 11) in that *everything* is negotiable. They are very different from seller carry backs in that the buyer never has title to the property until he or she acquires his or her own financing based on the terms of the agreement.

There are many terms to consider with the lease purchase acquisition strategy. The duration of the lease, purchase price, lease payments, rent credits, maintenance and repairs, and down-payment are all factors that can and should be negotiated to *your* satisfaction.

The duration of the lease purchase is infinite. It can be as short as a couple of months or as long as a couple of years. Generally, the longer the lease-purchase terms the better for you, the buyer. The thought being that the property can appreciate over the life of the agreement. For example, you agree on a 36-month lease-purchase on a $100,000 home. In an average market of six percent annual appreciation the same $100,000 property would be worth $119,101 in 36 months.

The caveat with this type of extended lease-purchase is that you *must* agree to lock in the *current* fair market value as the purchase price. This factor, more than any other, can make or break the benefits of a lease-purchase. The purchase price must not be based on a forecast of what the property will be worth in one, two, or three years. If this is the only option you have, then I suggest you entertain other options. There are hundreds of them out there.

Lease payments are another factor to be negotiated during the meeting of the minds. Generally, it is not wise to pay more than fair market rent unless you can get some of the other factors weighed in your favor. One of these factors would be the rent credit variable. This is the amount of your monthly payment that goes towards the down-payment when you purchase the property. At a minimum, this amount should not be less than ¼ of your monthly payment. So, if your monthly payment is $1000, $250 of that should go towards your down-payment as a rent credit.

Taking responsibility for repairs and maintenance is a great way to leverage your negotiating power and give the seller peace of mind. By assuming responsibility, you are able to communicate to the seller that he or she will no longer have to worry about their property. All that they have to do is go to the mailbox and pick up their rent check. Of course, this strategy is not recommended for an older property unless you get most or all of the other factors in your favor.

The down-payment or earnest deposit is a very significant factor that can be used to your advantage, if you are smart about it; ideally, the less money that you put down as earnest deposit for a lease-purchase the better. The reason for this is two fold: first, you want to leverage the transaction, and second, you don't want to bet the farm on something as unstable as a lease-purchase. This being said, by putting down a significant chuck of change of at least $5,000 on a $150,000 property you are able to make the seller feel better about other terms that lean in your favor as well as your sincerity to buy the property in the future and solve their problem.

A word of warning, there are some individuals (sellers) that make a living off of individuals (buyers) defaulting on lease purchases and forfeiting their earnest deposits. The *overwhelming* majority of lease-purchases are unsuccessful for the *buyer*. So the advice is that if you are going to enter into this type of acquisition strategy, make sure that you can, in fact, purchase the property on the date you have committed to do so.

LAND TRUSTS

Land trusts are a close relative to wrap around mortgages or FHA (Federal Housing Administration) and VA (Veteran's Administration) assumable loans. The general understanding is that the buyer takes over the payments for the seller's loan without having to qualify for the loan.

Wraps, as they are called, were much more popular before lenders began creating and enforcing due-on-sale clauses with their loans. A wrap enabled a buyer to "assume" an existing loan, conventional, FHA, VA, or otherwise, and "wrap" the payments and loan balance into a new loan that was created between the buyer and seller.

What this allowed the buyer and seller to do was to have the buyer take over the payments with or without a residual going to the seller, depending on how it was negotiated; the seller would transfer title to the buyer and the buyer would then just assume the property.

For understandable reasons, lending institutions were not crazy about wrap-around mortgages. From their perspective, they were giving a loan to somebody that may not have been qualified to have the loan in the first place. Lenders began to crack down on this process by instituting and enforcing due-on-sale clauses because many of their notes were being defaulted on. A due-on-sale clause allowed the lender to call the note due and payable if the property had been sold. Some investors still use this type of financing agreement, but they are hedging either on the lender not finding out about it and/or the lender enforcing the due-on-sale clause.

Once upon a time FHA and VA assumable loans were also this simple. A buyer could very easily sign on the dotted line and take over payments and title for the seller. These days are over. Enter the land trust.

Land trusts are fairly simple and similar to wrap-around mortgages or assumable loans. As with wraps and assumable loans, you need to find a homeowner that is willing to sell their property subject to the conditions. A land trust is then set up for the benefit of the seller. Title to the property is placed in the land trust. And then the seller would assign ownership of the trust to you, the buyer.

The land trust navigates around the due-on-sale clause because of two reasons. First by law, thanks to the Garn Act, the lender cannot do anything about a property being placed in the land trust. And second, the lender will have no knowledge that the seller has assigned ownership of the land trust to the buyer unless the buyer or seller tells the lender, which won't happen. The lender still continues to get their payments every month from the buyer.

Land trusts are a very simple way to take over payments on a property without having to qualify. The downside is that not all owners are willing to sell their property in this manner. I wanted to point this option out because this *may* be the only way that some buyers can get into a house when they are beginning their investing framework. Don't spend too much time thinking about this if you can qualify with other conventional manners. We will take an in depth look at more conventional and traditional acquisition strategies in Chapter 11, Other People's Money. This investing campaign is intended to be free from prospecting sellers for creative financing and various discounted properties.

REAL ESTATE MARKETS

Put very simply, there are three markets in real estate, the primary, secondary, and tertiary markets. These markets represent varying degrees of market exposure. All else being equal, there is a positive correlation between market exposure and the purchase price for a particular property. Very clearly, the more exposure a house receives, the higher the purchase price that property will sell for. What this law illustrates for buyers is that the best deals will be found in the secondary and tertiary markets. This being said, let me remind you that this book is about buying and holding. It is not about finding the deal of the century or any deals at all for that matter. *This information is intended only to create an awareness of the real estate markets; it is not intended to drive you to acquire properties in the secondary and tertiary markets.*

PRIMARY MARKET

The primary market is governed by real estate agents and brokers. These individuals understand the market value for a property and are committed to obtaining this value for the homeowners that they represent; they are professionals. If the agent or broker can't drive fair market value for a property they won't be in business for very long. To assist the homeowner to achieve fair market price, they use marketing campaigns to generate even more exposure outside of just the MLS or Multiple Listing Service. On a side note, it is also in their best interest to maximize the selling price for a property because they get paid more because they are paid on commissions. Although discounted houses can be found on the MLS, they are few and far between. One way of interpreting this market is to understand that properties are priced six percent above what they could be bought or sold for otherwise. This six percent is to accommodate for commission fees for real estate agents. Only the purchase price can be negotiated in this market; the fees attached to the price are rarely negotiated or reduced. Shopping this market is very time efficient but may not be very cost effective.

SECONDARY MARKET

The secondary market is made up FSBO's or For Sale by Owner's. The majority of these individuals are FSBO's because they do not want to or can't pay the six percent commissions that most homeowners in the primary market pay. What this allows you to do is to negotiate two factors instead of one. You can and should negotiate the commissions or lack there of *and* then the purchase price. More often than not, the buyer and seller agree to split the commissions so the buyer reduces the price by three percent and *then* negotiates the purchase price or value of the home. These savings do come at a significant cost in that it takes *much* more *time* to find the property with the terms you want than it would to find the same property in the primary market. The general rule of thumb is that if you want to buy properties in this market, you have to be willing to make multiple offers to get the terms you want.

If you are fortunate enough, you may be able to find distressed property owners that may be more committed to selling their property than other owners will be. These types of property owners may be in pre-foreclosure because they lost their job, be in the middle of a divorce, or have had a recent death in the family. Unfortunately, these are the types of sellers that you want to negotiate with.

A word of caution with acquiring properties in this market; odds are good that you will be working this market without a Realtor® or Real Estate Planner®; beware of paying too much for a "deal." By going it alone, you will not have the market knowledge that would prevent you from paying too much for a property. Never buy a property without doing a Comparative Market Analysis first.

TERTIARY MARKET

The tertiary market or wholesale market is where properties in some *rare* instances can be bought for up to

50 percent below fair market value; it is the equivalent of panning for gold. Only a few investors will be able to find and acquire these properties. These are houses that have already been foreclosed on. They are properties that are being sold by the county or by a bank. Bank-owned properties are commonly referred to as REO or real estate owned properties.

Let me make one distinction; there are many web sites and dealers that sell "foreclosed homes." These types of properties are not considered to be in the tertiary market but rather the *secondary* market because you are in essence dealing directly with an owner that has already bought the property at a foreclosure sale.

Here is an example as to how these work. Mr. and Mrs. Divorce lose their home in a foreclosure; their home is valued at $150,000. The home is auctioned off at the county courthouse. Mr. Greed buys the property for cash for $100,000. Mr. Greed then proceeds to put the house up for sale on his "foreclosure" web site and sell the house for $130,000. More often than not, Mr. Greed has not done any repairs or remodeling to the house; he is going to let you do that, for a price. So what we have here is a construction project. You are, in this example, able to purchase a property for 14 percent below market value from an owner, and *you* will have to make the lion's share of the repairs. If this is beginning to sound very much like the secondary or FSBO market, that is because it is.

Foreclosure specialists buy in the tertiary and sell in the secondary market to "investors" that for some reason or another enjoy construction projects.

The lesson to be learned about the tertiary market is this; if you are buying from a web site or a dealer or an owner or anyone other than a bank or the county, you are buying in the secondary market. It is that simple; do not be fooled. The reality of it is that there are many investors that do buy in the tertiary market and then resell the properties with the slimmest of margins to the secondary market to make it look lucrative. As you may have already learned or read about, these lucrative deals are very rarely lucrative. Think about it; why would an investor sell a perfect property to you at a 15-20 percent discount if they could sell it retail and get full price. They are not going to do you any free favors; everything comes at a cost.

The restriction to entering the tertiary market for buyers is that you need to have cash, and bundles of it. Because of this restriction, there are fewer buyers and thus less market exposure. This significant decrease in market exposure lends itself to properties selling for lower than normal market values. So, if you have cash or a line of credit, this *may* be a good place to acquire your properties. I say "*may*" because often times you are buying a property sight unseen. Many people have lost their shirt buying a foreclosed property. The reality of the tertiary market is that it is not what it used to be. Because of infomercials and an increase in awareness, more and more novice investors are showing up for amateur hour at the auction and paying *way* too much for a foreclosed property. This is why this framework is not designed for this type of property acquisition.

If you do unwisely decide to go against the recommendations in this book, you still need to know what you are going to do with the property in question. Do you "flip" it, in other words fix it up and immediately resell it, or do you hold on to it? In 99 percent of the scenarios the answer is pretty simple, hold on to it.

FLIPPING V. HOLDING

Here is the simple reason. In 99 percent of the acquisitions, the margin will not be significant enough to support the "flip" costs. Let's take a look and see how this works from a couple of different acquisition levels.

First, let me ask you a question; what is a good discount to get on a property? More often than not, most people will agree that a 20 percent discount is a fair place to start. The property we purchase has a market value of $100,000; we can acquire the property for $80,000, a 20 percent discount. Not bad, but not good either. Take a look at why these numbers and margin won't work.

Closing Costs (Buying):	$4,000
Improvements/Repairs:	$6,000
Carrying Costs (3 Months):	$2,000
Commissions:	$6,000
Closing Costs (Selling):	$1,000
Total Costs:	**$19,000**
Net Income before Tax:	**$1,000**
Capital Gains Taxes:	**$250**
Net Income after Tax:	**$750**

The closing costs when you purchase the property range anywhere from three to five percent of the purchase price; these costs also include your loan costs. This example shows the middle ground of $4,000.

The improvements and repairs include the most common expenses: carpet, paint, handyman hours for plumbing, electric, roofing, and all of the other minor cosmetic repairs that will need to be done. Utilities are another expense that are minor but they do add up; somebody has to pay for water and electricity to be turned on and provided to the house.

Carrying costs are an enormous unknown variable. This example shows three months of carrying costs; this is *very* conservative. Consider this, if doing these projects is not your full time job, it will take you at least a month for the repairs, more than likely two months before it is completely ready to be marketed. From this point, it will take anywhere from two to three months for the property to get a contract and another 30-45 days to close escrow, if that first offer does indeed even close. The reality of this is that you may be looking at five to seven months before you get your small check.

Commissions are another consideration. There are two ways to evaluate these, but only one makes sense. The first way, is to try to avoid paying the commissions and *try* to sell the home For Sale by Owner. What this equates to are bargain hunters and other investors putting in offers on your property, neither of which are a good thing for you and your margin. Not only will you not get near full price for the property, but it will also take you longer to sell, and thus costing you more carrying costs.

The communication with these types of scenarios usually goes a little something like this. The potential buyer will say, "I know you are not paying commissions, and I don't want to pay for them either. So why don't we take three percent off the price for starters." "Now that we have that settled, let's talk about the market value for your property, I'll give you 98 percent of market value."

So instead of getting full asking price for your property, realistically you are looking more in the range of $95,000-$96,000 by selling the property on your own, if you can sell it at all.

The second way to get the property or project sold is to list it with an agent. If you still insist on doing the fix-up or rehab properties despite all of the information you have been provided with, do yourself a favor and get a Realtor® or Real Estate Planner® to list the house for you. It will clearly save you time and money. Remember, you must have one of these on your team anyways.

Also don't forget about the closing costs that you will pay when you sell the property. They will be less than when you bought it, but it will still run you to the tune of one to two percent of the purchase price.

Lastly, Uncle Sam, you still need to pay him as well. Unlike income properties that are held for an extended period of time and can be sold via a 1031 tax deferred exchange so you don't need to pay Uncle Sam, the flipping or dealing of properties does not fall under the umbrella of a 1031 exchange. This means that you will probably be paying out about 25 percent of your gain to the government.

So after it is all said and done, after it took you a couple of weeks or even months to find the "deal of the century," spent weeks or months fixing the property yourself or meeting contractors to fix it for you, having the property on the market for a couple of months, and another 30-45 days of escrow, you get paid a lousy $750. If you were to take this $750 and divide it by the number of hours you put into the construction project, you would be better off claiming unemployment.

Understand this; you are buying a construction project, not an investment or income property. When it is all said and done, this construction project took from beginning, finding the property, to end, closing escrow, anywhere between five to seven months for a part timer. Was it worth it?

The likelihood of these types of projects working out for you, and your getting paid what you are worth, are very slim. These projects *were* more profitable back in the 70's, 80's and even early 90's. However, due to the information age we are now in, everybody and their cousin is aware of the market; there is more competition, and this competition is driving the prices for these projects through the roof. You have probably already seen it on street corners and in the newspaper, "I buy homes cash," or "I buy houses."

This is your competition; they are professionals, and they are everywhere. The only way for you to compete is to quit your job, get a line of cash for a couple hundred thousand, and work like hell. Or you can read on and follow the framework that is provided in this book.

The alternative to "flipping" the property would be to fix it up and *rent* it. In this example you will save yourself over $9,000 and change because you don't have the extended carrying costs, commissions, closing costs on the back end, or the capital gain taxes. Instead, you have a property with about $10,000 of instant equity in addition to whatever initial investment you may have already had to put down on the property. This is a much more lucrative decision for the framework that we are working within.

If this result or financing structure still is not satisfactory to you, you could take out a 2nd mortgage or a line of credit, or even refinance the whole project to get some of your "profit" or equity out of the project so that you could maximize your return on equity and reduce your potential tax obligation (Warning: FHA guidelines are now prohibiting early loan pay-offs specifically because of these types of projects). In this scenario, the profit would be tax free because you have not sold the property, you have refinanced. Refinancing is a tax-free transaction. Hopefully, some lights are going on and the recommendations and rules of the game are beginning to make sense for you, this is just the tip of the iceberg.

Finally, and most importantly, this framework was designed so you can leverage your *time*. Time is your most precious resource. This framework was designed so that you don't have to continually "pan" for the next great deal. It was designed so that you will be financially independent in 10 years. Looking for properties that are truly wholesale properties requires not only an *ongoing* time commitment but it also is not a strategy that is going to work for *everybody all* of the time. This "strategy" of acquiring properties wholesale is a strategy that is doomed. Not only does it not provide consistent results, but there is no definitive end or time frame for the framework. In other words, after 10 years of wholesaling properties, you will *still* be wholesaling properties. In addition, the wholesaling of properties does not allow you to create massive and most importantly *legal* tax shelters. In fact, the capital gain that you experience will more than likely be taxed as such, further eating into your profit margins.

HOLDING PROPERTY

Holding strategies are the third concept we will discuss in this chapter. Holding strategies can be in the form of a single person or multiple people. The bottom line is that there needs to be a very careful and pre-meditated plan for holding your properties. Ideally, you control everything but own nothing.

Along with all of the incredible financial benefits, real estate investing comes with an equal dose of liability and *tax opportunities*. Your accountant's or attorney's job is to determine the best holding strategy for *you* so that you can not only limit your liability but also decrease your potential tax obligation. This holding strategy can come in several forms, a sole proprietorship, partnership, an LLC, a corporation, or even a trust.

Because each individual has different financial circumstances and needs, as well as the complexity of the subject matter, I will not bore nor complicate you with the pros and cons for each type of holding structure. Instead, I will strongly recommend you hire a professional for your team to do this. However, do understand that each type of holding structure will have very clear differences in regards to tax obligation, liability exposure, and various monetary and legal requirements.

INTEREST RATES

The "x" factor that has an influence on *all* of the acquisition strategies that have been mentioned in this chapter are the interest rates. Interest rates effect not only buying power but also market price. The only time interest rates are not *as* significant of a factor is when you buy and hold properties in the form of cash, which is not recommended, and even then rates can and still do have an influence on the acquisition price.

The interest rates determine how much buying power you have or, in other words, how much of an asset you can acquire. So if interest rates are low, you have a strong buying power; if interest rates are high, you have a weak buying power. The higher the interest rates, the larger the monthly payment; the lower the interest rates, the smaller the monthly payment. The common denominator is debt service.

Large payments equal a higher debt to income ratio. Smaller payments equal a lower debt to income ratio. Clearly from a lending perspective, which is most often the only perspective that counts, the debt to income ratio needs to work for the specific loan product or the loan can not be approved.

Another way to look at interest rates is to look at them as the cost of money. Basically, the rates tell you how cheap or expensive money is to borrow. This is important when you analyze whether or not to move forward with an acquisition. So if it costs you 15 percent to get the money and you are only making 10 percent on a return annually, it *may* not be a prudent investment. Remember, there are other factors like cash flow and tax write-offs that should also be factored into the equation. On the other hand, if you can get money like you can today at six percent and generate 20-30 percent annually, clearly it makes good financial sense to move forward.

Interest rates also influence market price for properties. As interest rates, decline more people want to buy real estate. The majority of people buy for one of three reasons in this type of market. They either want a larger home, a 2nd home or investment property, or they are a first time home buyer. The bottom line is there is an increase in demand for people buying real estate. This demand drives housing prices up leading to a soft buying market. So, although purchasing power is increased, the market price is also inflated.

During a hike in interest rates, less people are purchasing real estate. Fewer people are able to buy larger homes, investment properties become not so popular, and would be first-time home buyers can no longer qualify. These factors lend themselves to a decrease in demand and a hard buyers market. In short, housing prices remain stable or may in some instances decrease.

> *"There is only one good, knowledge, and one evil, ignorance."*
>
> *Socrates*

POINTS TO REMEMBER: ACQUISITION STRATEGIES

1.) Lease Purchases or rent-to-owns are very similar to that of a seller carry back (Chapter 11) in that *everything* is negotiable. They are very different from seller carry backs in that the buyer never has title to the property until he or she acquires his or her own financing based on the terms of the agreement.

2.) Land trusts are a close relative to wrap around mortgages or FHA and VA assumable loans. The general understanding is that the buyer takes over payments for the seller's loan without having to qualify.

3.) These financing techniques allow you to purchase or acquire properties in the primary, secondary, and tertiary housing markets. These markets represent respectively, first, MLS listed properties, second, FSBO's or distressed properties, and third, foreclosures and REO properties.

4.) In 99 percent of the "discounted" acquisitions the margin will not be significant enough to support the "flip" costs of a property. You are better off holding properties for the long term.

5.) There needs to be a very careful and thought out plan for holding your properties. Ideally, you control everything but own nothing.

6.) The "x" factor that has an influence on *all* of the acquisition strategies that have been mentioned in this chapter are the interest rates. Interest rates effect not only buying power but also market price.

CHAPTER 7
LEARN THE BUSINESS

"Good judgment comes from experience, and experience comes from bad judgment."

Barry LePatner

As with any other business endeavor it is critical for you, the business owner, to understand how the business lives and breathes. It is important to understand and see the cash coming in and going out. The biggest mistake a lot of real estate investors make is that they don't treat their investments like a business, and because of this they don't understand how it works or how to make money. Although it is important to focus on the long-term plan rather than the immediate cash flow situation, it is also critical to make sure that your company is at least breaking on an annual basis even in the short term.

A business like amazon.com may be able to get away with red cash flow in the short term because they are a public company and stockholders continue to invest with them. Your business on the other hand is a private company without investors; treat it accordingly. Once you run out of money, you are out of business; it is that simple.

Just as a new business owner would plan, prepare, and analyze monthly and yearly figures for their business, you need to do the same. Every penny that comes in and out of the business needs to be analyzed before, during, and after each month. You need to understand the equations that drive your business, to understand where your money is won and lost, and how you can maximize the gains and minimize the losses. This is what you will learn in this chapter. Pay attention, get the highlighter, and take notes.

There are seven steps that must be performed when running an efficient and profitable property holding business. First, a Comparative or Competitive Market Analysis or CMA needs to be performed and evaluated. Second, a Rental Comparative Market Analysis or RCMA needs to be researched. Third, a Monthly Cash Flow Analysis must be calculated before property acquisition. Fourth, an Annual Financial Forecast allows you to project the performance of the property 10 years into the future. Fifth, a Monthly Profit & Loss Statement needs to be recorded, tracked, and analyzed each month. Sixth, a cash reserve account needs to be established and managed. And finally, getting a tenant into the property and managing the investment.

COMPARATIVE MARKET ANALYSIS (CMA)

The Comparative Market Analysis or CMA is the first and most important step for analyzing a property before the acquisition. Basically what a CMA does is take a snapshot of all of the activity in a particular neighborhood or area for a particular floor plan, property model, or house with similar square feet. The market activity is commonly over a six-month period.

The CMA has two purposes. First, the comparative part of the CMA allows you to compare what other homes have sold for in the neighborhood. This is critical because it very clearly illustrates what a home will appraise for and thus tells you what amount a lending institution will give you a loan for. The gauge for this is to measure the value of the property in dollars per square foot.

On a side note, the appraisal is a requirement for any house that you plan on financing with a mortgage. The purpose of the appraisal is to ensure that the mortgage you have given to the lending institution is at least equal to the value of the house and not more than the house. The reason this is important is because the lending institution wants to be certain that if they need to foreclose on the property and take the property back, that they can recoup their losses.

There are some circumstances where a lending institution will actually lend for 105 or 110 percent value of the house, but we will not go into those circumstances right now.

The interesting thing about appraisals is that they safeguard your investment so that you do not pay more than fair market value for your property. In essence, you can't buy "high", so to speak, like you can with overvalued and inflated stocks.

If an appraisal could have been performed in April of 2000 on various equities in the stock market, many people would have saved a lot of money and a lot of heartache by ceasing to buy stocks at a value higher than what the company or stock was truly worth.

One caveat to be aware of is that appraisals are driven by two factors, the CMA and the appraiser. What this infers is that they are part science and part art form; in essence, they are part subjective in nature. There is room for human error and interpretation. You could have five different appraisers come out and look at the same property on the same day and get five different, yet approximate, property values. In fact, what drives most appraisal values is the purchase contract price. If an appraiser has a price they need to meet, and that price is in the ball park of the other comparables, more often than not the desired price will be met.

The second part of the CMA is known as the *Competitive* Market Analysis because it shows what the competition or other houses are *currently listed* for in the same neighborhood or area.

The reality of the housing market is that the home sellers are selling a product. Often times and understandably so, emotions get involved and they begin to think that they are selling memories and pride of ownership. This often skews their perception of the value of their house. The competitive market analysis allows these types of sellers to hopefully be brought back from fantasy land to reality. The reason this is significant is because the home sellers become aware that their house, or the product they are selling, has competition, the competition being the other houses in the neighborhood that are also for sale.

Clearly, all else being equal, an educated buyer will not buy a house for $155,000 when they could get the same or similar property for $150,000. Once the purchaser becomes educated about the other houses on the market, it allows him or her to negotiate the price on several properties.

Hopefully you can see that this type of information can lead to a buyer's market. A buyer's market is indicative of a buyer running the game. The buyer, not the seller, dictates what they will pay for a home. This is a matter of submitting multiple offers on multiple properties over a period of time. The end result is that the buyer does not *need* to buy; and eventually the buyer will find a seller that *needs* to sell, yesterday. This type of equation results in an acquisition at below retail value.

More often than not, most real estate markets are buyer's markets. The general exception to this rule is when there are fewer houses on the market than there are qualified buyers looking to acquire properties. This type of environment or seller's market occur when there is a very desirable area with limited or no room to build and for some reason or another, likely due to a booming local economy, no home owners want to sell. The result is a very quick acceleration in property values or appreciation that is eventually followed by a just as quick depreciation in property values. In other words the real estate bubble bursts. It is important to note that this type of seller's market is almost exclusively limited to specific communities or cities and are not common as a national trend. If you are investing or living in one of these areas it would be very wise to hedge your investments by also acquiring properties that are not located in the same area. Don't have all your eggs in one basket if the basket is attached to a helium balloon.

With the right tools there are almost unlimited opportunities for buyers to acquire properties at below retail or wholesale prices. *The framework of this book and the strategies involved are not based on wholesale property acquisition but rather retail property acquisition. Any property that is acquired below retail is a bonus for this real estate framework.*

The CMA is the first step to getting a hold on and understanding your business. You are buying a product; it is that simple. You are acquiring inventory that at some point in time, hopefully in exactly 10 years if you are following the framework, you will be reselling. It is imperative that you do not pay more than is necessary to acquire the product. This point is the purpose of the CMA.

RENTAL COMPARATIVE MARKET ANALYSIS (RCMA)

If we have arrived at this step it means we have narrowed down the property search to a specific house and price point. The next step, step two, is to determine what we can rent the property for.

Before we go any further it needs to be disclosed that *every* property can be rented. It is the rental price that will vary massively depending upon the location and appearance of the house as well as the terms of the lease or rental agreement. Even a shanty, although perhaps not legally, can be rented out to a homeless person. So remember, just like selling a house, pricing and marketing are everything when it comes time to rent your investment property. This will be illustrated a bit later in this chapter; for now we want to know what properties have been rented recently and what properties are currently for rent; this is the purpose of the RCMA.

Hopefully you understand that the Rental Comparative Market Analysis or RCMA is very similar to that of the CMA that we had just discussed.

The first part of the RCMA is the equivalent to the first part of the CMA in that it shows what properties have been *renting* for in the past six months or a year. The appropriate gauge for this measurement is dollars per square foot. In this way it is similar to the CMA. It is unique from the CMA in that the gross rent should be totaled over the year.

Here is an example; if you have a 1200 square foot house that rents for $1000 a month or $12,000 a year, the dollar per square foot would equal $10 per square foot. This is the measurement by which commercial properties can be valued. Begin to look at the value of your property by the amount of gross income it generates per annum per square foot of the property. This data will allow you to see what properties are generating the most income per size. I can not emphasize this enough; treat this framework like a business.

Unlike the CMA, the RCMA does not have an appraisal that drives the selling price or in this case the rental price for a rental property. All else being equal, the rental price is the average price that you could rent your property for. This rental amount is important for step three, the Monthly Cash Flow Analysis.

What is more important for this analysis is the second part of the RCMA. The second part will show the properties that are currently on the market for rent. This is significant because this is the competition you have for getting your property rented. Again, the comparison can be made that you are selling or renting/leasing a product, your investment property; you *must* consider what the market dictates, *not* what *you* would like to rent the property for. Obviously, all else being equal, a renter will choose the least expensive property to rent.

It is also notable that just as most markets are buyer's markets in the resale housing market, most markets are renter's markets in the rental market.

As a rule of thumb, you want to have one of the least expensive rental properties on the market. The logic is very simple; we have already determined it is a renter's market; if you can't get the property rented as soon as possible, you will pay double mortgages until you can get it rented.

Common sense and personal experience will tell you that you are better off taking a cut of $100 or $150 to get your property rented immediately than to wait two or three months to get your asking price.

For example, the market rent dictates that you can rent your $150,000 property for between $1050 and $1150 a month, a $100 difference that would add up to an extra $1200 over the course of the year. This being said, if you could get the property to rent six weeks earlier for $1050 instead of $1150, it would be in your best interest to do so. We are thinking about gross rental income; think big picture.

$1050 x 12 months = $12,600 $1150 x 10.5 months = $12,075

From personal experience, if a tenant offers you a rental price in the range of where you find it acceptable and they are qualified, move forward with it because you are not sure when the next tenant will be coming by. Don't lose a tenant over $100 a month. Think long term and think occupancy.

The simple rule is occupancy, not cash flow, is king. When you think annual cash flow as opposed to monthly cash flow, the decision becomes very obvious. As long as they can pay your mortgage and you can still be in the black, you will be in good shape. Remember, you choose to invest in real estate because of two reasons, to maximize your return on equity and to reduce your potential tax obligation. You are not investing in real estate to generate massive *taxable* cash flow or to pay *multiple* mortgages on your own so you can really have some great write-offs at the end of the year.

MONTHLY CASH FLOW ANALYSIS

The Monthly Cash Flow Analysis allows an investor to see how the property or business will perform over the 12 months moving forward. The necessity of this type of forecast is that it allows you to anticipate the costs associated with the property, and then from this, you can make financing or acquisition adjustments so that you can produce the desired cash flow for the property.

The most efficient and financially scientific way to perform this type of analysis is to purchase the REP® software at TheNewGoldRush.biz. This software allows you to produce various cash flow scenarios in a very short period of time. It allows you to adjust interest rate assumptions, initial investment costs, vacancies, management costs, and maintenance costs so that you can determine best and worst case scenarios for cash flow for a specific property. This way you can plan for the worst, and ideally there will not be any surprises for the investment.

If you do decide to move forward with your investing and you have decided to treat it like a business, get the REP® software; it is the appropriate next step. Just as you would evaluate your portfolio statement from your financial advisor or financial planner, you should also evaluate your real estate portfolio. Again, what gets managed and measured is what you can improve upon. If you are not measuring or managing it, you can't improve it.

ANNUAL FINANCIAL FORECAST

"Do not worry about your problems with mathematics. I assure you mine are still greater."

Albert Einstein

There are several figures that your Annual Financial Forecast should keep track of. These measurements include return on equity, return on investment, possible tax deductions, principal and interest payments, and CAP Rates.

Return on equity is a very significant measurement in that it shows you how hard your equity is working, or in other words, what your equity is producing. The longer you stay in a property without refinancing, the smaller your return on equity will be for the years moving forward. It is critical to watch this very closely in your personal residence.

Return on investment is a calculation that shows the return you have received on your initial down-payment and closing costs. This number will continue to grow over the years moving forward due to the power of compounding.

The possible tax deductions are a combination of the cost of business expenses like management, insurance, taxes, repairs, HOA fees, and most importantly depreciation.

The principal and interest payments will vary depending on the type of loan that you use to acquire the property. Mortgages like ARMs or interest-only loans will produce significant changes in monthly payments when compared to a 30-year fixed loan. These changes should be planned for ahead of time.

The CAP Rate or Capitalization Rate is a number that is determined by using the gross income relative to the value of the property. In short, the value of a property is equal to the gross income divided by the CAP Rate. Or in other words, the CAP Rate is equal to gross income divided by the value of the property. This is a number that should also be watched closely if your investing framework places a large emphasis on cash flow. The lower the CAP Rate the less cash flow that will be generated relative to the value of the property. The higher the CAP Rate, the more cash flow that will be generated relative to the value of the property.

A common occurrence is for the *lower valued* properties to produce higher CAP Rates than higher valued properties.

The REP® software is the tool that you use to analyze your investments before, during, and after you make them. If you are not using it, you are losing money; it is that simple.

MONTHLY PROFIT & LOSS STATEMENT

Up to this point we have talked about the value of the property (CMA), the surrounding rental market (RCMA), the projected Monthly Cash Flow Analysis, and the Annual Financial Forecast. We have done our homework and have made decisions as to how we are going to structure the property acquisition. It is now time to manage the business with a Monthly Profit & Loss Statement.

This enables the owner or Real Estate Planner® to watch the business on a monthly schedule just as you would watch any other business. Doing this allows you to make changes that need to be made. One of these changes would include purchasing a home warranty if the property is not under a builder warranty and it is beginning to show signs of wear.

A home warranty can be very important and at the same time very misunderstood. A home warranty is very common when you buy a property resale. What a lot of people do not realize is that home warranties are renewable, at cost, and they can even be placed on a house that you have owned that does not currently have a warranty plan on it. So for about $350 you can get an "insurance policy" on *repairs* that may need to be made to your property. These policies do not provide 100 percent coverage nor are they free from service fees, but they do help to keep enormous and unexpected repairs to a minimum. The chances are that at some point in the life of your investment property you will need some type of major repair or replacement done, or at the minimum, you will have several smaller service repairs; use the home warranty to hedge against these costs. In most instances it will more than pay for itself. At the least, hopefully you can rest better at night knowing you do have a system in place to deal with property repairs.

Some other month to month financial areas to watch would include the management expenses, HOA fees, advertising costs if the property is vacant, as well as increases in taxes and insurance. These items have a tendency to sneak up on you and to add up very quickly if you are not paying attention.

RESERVES

One very important note that needs to be recognized is the importance of having reserves for each property. So as not to look like the North end of a South bound horse, at a minimum, a three-month mortgage reserve must be maintained for the life of each property.

The mortgage reserve should be based on a 100 percent loan payment. So if you have a $100,000 property you should have about $1,900 in reserves (3 x $628), regardless of your actual mortgage payment. What is the significance of three months? A couple of reasons; first, you are not certain how long it will take to get the property rented. Second, you want to be prepared for unforeseen repairs that need to be performed. And third, and hopefully if the tenant has been professionally screened, this will never happen; you may need the reserves if the tenant ceases to pay rent yet still feels comfortable continuing to live in your property. Evictions will usually take a couple of months depending on the state that the property is located in.

Think of these reserves as a rainy day fund. When is the best time to repair a roof, when it is sunny of course? Likewise, the best time to prepare for a financial shortage or emergency is when there is no financial emergency.

To Manage Or Not To Manage?

Getting a tenant into your property and managing the property is the last step. Depending on the market, finding a tenant can be easier said than done. A general rule is the lower the interest rates, the softer the rental market, and thus more vacancies for your properties. The management responsibilities for the months moving forward once you do find a tenant is also something to consider.

The reasons a soft market makes it difficult to find a tenant are two-fold and it is driven by both ends of the market. On the tenant side of things, the lower the interest rate, the easier it is for them to qualify and purchase their own home as opposed to renting. On the other side of the equation are the investors. The lower the interest rate is, the more investors there will be in the market, and thus the more rental properties in the market. As the interest rates rise, fewer and fewer investors will be entering the market. This type of environment tends to separate the professional long-term investor from the amateur dabbler.

All of this being said, it would take *very* rare circumstances for it *not* to make sense to invest in the real estate market.

As long as the acquisition is structured properly, real estate will always be the best investment you can ever make.

Effective marketing is critical to getting your property leased. It is not necessarily how many dollars that are spent advertising but rather *where* the dollars are spent. It is not necessarily how much you do, but rather what you do. The most effective strategy is to use the "For Rent" sign posts that can be stapled to a stake and hammered into the ground. It is *very* cost effective and the exposure is incredible. For $40 you can target and blanket a large area with 10 signs and it will generate many more leads than any print advertising could ever do. And the best part is that it is targeted or geographical advertising. You only get calls from people who want to live in the area that you are advertising in.

The MLS or Multiple Listing Service is another tool that can be used to market a rental property; but experience has shown that very few tenants will call a Realtor® to find them a house to rent. Most of these potential tenants will work alone. Although there are Realtors® that specialize in finding properties to rent, the vast majority of tenants think of Realtors® as working the retail market as opposed to the rental market.

Section 8 housing is another factor to consider when marketing your property. Section 8 housing assistance comes in the form of the government subsidizing a low-income tenant's rent payments. The tenant may pay up to 30 percent of household income and the remaining balance is paid by the housing authority directly to the landlord. The only caveat to this is that the rent you charge cannot exceed HUD's fair market rents for the area. If it does, the tenant would have to pick up the balance in addition to the percent share they were already paying. Section 8 housing truly is a win-win. You procure a tenant while at the same time you provide better and more affordable housing than the tenant would have been able to find had they not gone through Section 8. You can contact your city housing department to find out more information as to how to market your property to Section 8 tenants.

One last consideration in regards to procuring a tenant, think about what is most efficient when servicing and showing your properties. It is most efficient to select four or five subdivisions that are close in proximity to farm for rentals. This way you can have multiple properties, two or three, in one division and you will have a much more streamlined system. In essence it allows you to turn your single family houses into multiple family properties in terms of maintenance and showings.

The decision to manage your property can be answered very easily. Try it yourself for as long as it takes you to realize that you don't want to do it, and then farm it out. Remember, you are running a business. In order for that business to run smoothly and more importantly be profitable, the business owner, you, has to understand the business. You have to understand the value of a good property management company, and the cost of a bad one. Ultimately, once you acquire a couple of properties you will need to hire out, but before you do that you should understand how things work. These things include, showing the rental, screening the tenants, filling out the paperwork, invoicing the tenants, and most importantly, where are your expenses going to. If you want to know what is going on with your company, then you have to follow one very simple rule, sign every check.

The investment for management services is usually between eight to ten percent of the gross monthly rent. This may seem like a large chuck of change; but when you consider you are not investing exclusively for cash flow, and that you still have your day job, it is clearly in your best interest to let a professional handle the responsibilities. This way you act as a "silent" partner. You won't get any calls, or have to make any trips to the property; all you have to do is go to the mailbox and pick up your check once a month. Remember, this framework is about leverage;

why should you do it when you can pay a professional to do it.

> *"Experience is a hard teacher because she gives the test first, the lesson afterwards."*
>
> *Vernon Sanders Law*

POINTS TO REMEMBER: LEARN THE BUSINESS

1.) Just as a new business owner would plan, prepare, and analyze monthly and yearly figures for their business, you need to do the same.

2.) There are seven steps that must be performed when running an efficient and profitable property holding business. First, a Comparative or Competitive Market Analysis or CMA needs to be performed and evaluated. Second, a Rental Comparative Market Analysis or RCMA needs to be researched. Third, a Monthly Cash Flow Analysis must be calculated before property acquisition. Fourth, an Annual Financial Forecast allows you to project the performance of the property 10 years into the future. Fifth, a Monthly Profit & Loss Statement needs to be recorded, tracked, and analyzed each month. Sixth, a cash reserve account needs to be established and managed. And finally, getting a tenant into the property and managing the investment.

3.) The Comparative Market Analysis or CMA is the first and most important step for analyzing a property before the acquisition stage. It tells you what the competition is selling their properties for and how much the property will appraise for.

4.) The RCMA is very similar to that of the CMA. It shows what competition you have getting your property rented and what other properties have rented for in the past six months.

5.) The Monthly Cash Flow Analysis allows an investor to see how the property or business will perform over the 12 months moving forward. The necessity of this type of forecast is that it allows you to anticipate the costs associated with the property and then from this you can make financing or acquisition adjustments so that you can produce the desired cash flow for the property.

6.) There are several figures that your Annual Financial Forecast should keep track of. These measurements include return on equity, return on investment, possible tax deductions, principal and interest payments, and CAP Rates.

7.) The Monthly Profit and Loss Statement enables the owner or Real Estate Planner to watch the business on a monthly schedule to see how the property is producing as compared to the projections.

8.) So as not to look like the North end of a South bound horse, at a minimum, a three-month mortgage reserve must be maintained for the life of each property.

9.) Getting a tenant into your property is the last step. Depending on the market, this can be easier said than done. A general rule is the lower the interest rates, the softer the rental market and thus more vacancies for your properties.

CHAPTER 8
ONE GIANT STEP – FROM INVESTMENT TO INCOME PROPERTIES

"In the truest sense, freedom cannot be bestowed; it must be achieved."

Franklin D. Roosevelt

If you have read this far, you should understand that you are starting a business and the job of that business is to maximize your return on equity and to reduce your potential tax obligation. The first 10 years of the framework have allowed you to acquire assets, grow your equity tax free, and to understand the business. You now have two primary investment options made available to you for the years moving forward.

The first option is that you can perpetuate the previous growth cycle but this time instead of acquiring one property a year for ten years, you can acquire two to four properties a year for ten years. This increase in property acquisition is derived from the equity you are able to build up in your first 10 properties during the first 10 years.

The second alternative you have after the first 10-year period is to focus your attention on easing the management responsibilities and create consistent cash flow as opposed to growth; this concept is the basis of this chapter.

Before we move on, it is important to make a clarification on these two types of properties or alternatives and their financing structures.

WORKHORSE V. RACEHORSE (INVESTMENT PROPERTY VS. INCOME PROPERTY)

Up to now we have discussed various acquisition and wealth building strategies; these strategies are intended for those individuals that are looking to build wealth over a 10-year period and are not concerned with massive monthly cash flow in the immediate future. These individuals acquire properties and structure financing for two reasons, to take advantage of massive investment returns and to minimize their potential tax obligation. "Workhorse" or investment properties are the terms for these types of financing structures.

They perform just like they sound; they are persistent, consistent, and very powerful. You want to have a bunch of these in your stables; they do the dirty work and produce results over the long haul. It may not seem like they are performing; in fact they can be compared to watching grass grow, but they do grow, massively, if you give them time. This type of investing framework can be termed trickle-up investing.

The "racehorse" or income property is a property that is very different from the workhorse. These are properties that have a very strong equity position and produce massive cash flow. They perform very well on a month-to-month basis but they don't do much to grow your wealth over an extended period of time or to minimize your tax bill. They produce counter to the "workhorse." As we will discuss in the chapters moving forward, there is a time and a place for these properties.

CASH IS NOT KING

It is very important that I make a distinction with the workhorse vs. racehorse comparison. Much has been said about the importance of cash flow, and while cash flow certainly is important, it should not be a driving force during the early stages of wealth accumulation.

One ideology is that once you create enough passive cash flow to cover your monthly living expenses, you can retire. Although there is some truth to this, this scenario presumes that you are content with your current standard of living. Chances are if you are in lower to middle class economic standing, you will not be content to live the rest of your life in the house you currently own, driving the cars you drive, and taking the same vacations if you are able to take any at all.

Early on, it is critical to acquire workhorse properties; then after accumulating the wealth you desire, you can structure these properties or acquire other properties for the racehorse or cash flow mentality. It is similar in some regard to investing in the stock market. The sooner you begin putting money into stocks, the longer the time these stocks have to grow and compound. If you start much later in life, the stocks will still grow but because they have not had time to compound, the returns will be much more insignificant. Take advantage of leverage early on and you will be home free sooner than you think.

For example, let's take a look at the *value* of an additional $1,000 down-payment over a 10-year term. *On average a thousand dollars will decrease your debt service by about $7 a month.* At this rate, it would take over 142 months to get your thousand dollars back via cash flow. This is close to 12 years! In short, if you don't have to put down additional money to acquire a property, don't.

It is also important to mention that the additional thousand dollars will decrease your return on investment and your return on equity in addition to increasing your tax base for the years moving forward. So in essence, if you create $7 more a month in passive cash flow, you will be taxed on it. So that $7 is really closer to $4.70 that you take home, all else being equal. This would push the break-even scenario out to over 213 months or close to 18 years! If you want to grow your wealth, tax free, and in the shortest amount of time possible, cash flow is *not* king.

A more financially prudent decision would be to use that extra $1,000 as a partial down-payment on a 2nd property. This way you can obtain an additional asset that will provide massive returns on equity and enormous opportunities for tax-write-offs.

ONE GIANT STEP

Now that we are clear about the reality of cash flow, we do need to examine at what point it *does* make sense to structure your business to generate passive cash flow. You have two options after the first 10-year cycle. You can perpetuate the cycle again and create even more massive amounts of equity, or you can create a life-long stream of passive income.

By perpetuating the investment cycle again, you will be able to acquire two to four properties a year based on the previous 10 years of capital or equity build up.

For example, in the 10th year of holding a property, you should have close to $138,000 in equity within the house. We assume that we bought the property for $150,000 in the 1st year. The $150,000 property would be worth about $268,000 in the 10th year based on six percent annual appreciation. The $138,000 in equity is a combination of both debt reduction (approximately $20,000 over 10 years) as well as appreciation (approximately $118,000 over 10 years). We can then perform a 1031 exchange on the original property and theoretically acquire four properties each with 10 percent down. So if the median property value in 10 years is $268,000 and we need 10 percent for a down-payment, we would need approximately $26,800 to acquire one property or $107,200 to acquire four properties. You would still have a remainder of $21,000 to pay for closing costs, buy a 5th property, or have a stronger equity position in the four new properties.

This framework would lend itself to 40 properties in a 20-year time frame. Also remember that it would take none of your own money out of your savings or retirement funds to make this jump from 10 properties to 40 properties in 10 years.

If you are young and ambitious, this strategy may be the one for you. It will take a longer period of time, but at the end of the second 10-year cycle you will own anywhere from 20 to 40 properties, easily, and you will be growing your equity at an incredible rate. What this may not do for you is make you liquid or feel secure. Clearly, if you have multiple highly leveraged properties, you will not generate massive cash flow, and you will not very easily be able to access your equity should you need to get at it. Again, this is great for growth but at the same time it leaves you stretched thin and inflexible.

The second alternative, the topic of this chapter, allows for *massive* passive cash flow. The best way to do this is to structure your properties so that you have a strong equity position that will allow it to generate greater cash flow due to the decrease in debt service. This type of investment structure holds a couple of options. You can either hold on to the 10 residential properties you have and allow them to generate larger and larger cash flow for the years moving forward, or you can think instead about acquiring a commercial property like an apartment building, office space, or perhaps mini-storage units with a strong equity position.

Although it is possible to generate cash flow via residential income properties, there are a couple of deterrents to this strategy; they include the geographical area, the quality of tenants, and the number of tenants.

First, the management is much more encumbering with residential properties because the properties are likely strewn across a fairly large geographical area. Obviously with an apartment complex, office building, or storage building, all of your tenants are in one place.

Second, it is also important to look at the quality of tenants that you are leasing your property to. Clearly, there will be a significant difference between a tenant in an income property versus a tenant in Class A office space, or better yet, even storage space. This means payments will be made on time, there is less of an opportunity for damage being done to your property, and fewer phone calls will be made to you or your property manager.

Third, the number of tenants is also a concern. There is an opportunity to experience a much more *consistent* cash flow each and every month when you have multiple tenants or units. Clearly, the more units you have the less variance you will experience in gross income. If you have 10 units and two are vacant, you lose 20 percent of your income. On the other-hand if you have 20 units and two are vacant, you only lose 10 percent of your income. This rational lends itself to an apartment complex or storage units.

The reality of the situation is that every investor is going to feel differently about different types of investments. You have to do what is most prudent for you. As you have learned, there are clearly management and consistent cash flow benefits to commercial properties; but there are also tax and investment advantages to residential properties.

A general rule of thumb is that if you have been investing residential, and it has been successful for you, you should keep your assets in that market. If you have been investing residential and you want a more secure and safe investment, then you would want to transfer your assets into commercial. And lastly, if you have accumulated your wealth outside of real estate and you want to jump into real estate for the first time, it would be best that you acquire commercial properties versus residential properties. Clearly an individual in this type of equitable position would not want to go out and acquire 10 *vacant,* single family income properties if they could instead acquire an apartment complex, office space, or mini-storage that would generate instant cash flow for them.

Although commercial properties can generate more *consistent* cash flow based on a greater volume of tenants, the terms of the commercial loans and the tax write-off opportunities made available by the IRS, make commercial properties in some respects, much less long-term financially desirable than residential properties.

A commercial property is any property that is zoned commercial or it is a property that has greater than four residential units in one building. So a 4-plex would fall under residential financing and a 5-plex would fall under commercial financing.

Let's take a look at an example of some office space and see how the cash flow, the return on equity, and the depreciation opportunities it generates compares to that of residential properties. We will assume the office space is purchased for $450,000 and the three residential properties are each purchased for $150,000 (a total of $450,000).

To keep it simple, we will assume that each type of property generates a nine percent CAP rate; we are not going to include repairs or any other expenses; we are just looking at gross income. This means that the $450,000 commercial property will generate $40,500 in gross income a year. The three residential properties would also generate this same amount of gross income. *The variance in monthly cash flow comes from the commitment to debt service.* The commercial properties require a minimum of 25 percent down as opposed to the residential property that requires only 10 percent down (there are programs for five percent as well).

The $450,000 property would have a loan for $337,500 or 75 percent of the value of the property. The payments would be $2,371 principal and interest a month over a 25-year term at seven percent interest. Commercial loans are commonly amortized over a period of 20-25 years with a balloon payment at the 5 or 10 year mark.

The three residential properties would have a combined loan value of $405,000 or 90 percent of the value of the properties. The payments would be $2,678 principal and interest a month over a 30-year term at seven percent interest.

The difference in monthly cash flow between the commercial property and residential properties is $307 a month in favor of the commercial property. However, the commercial property required an additional $67,500 as down-payment. This means it would take close to 220 months or over 18 years to get that $67,500 back in our wallet via passive monthly cash flow. This is a decision that you have to make; every investor has different needs at different times.

Now we will look at the return on equity. Due to lending guidelines, we will be required to put down at least a 25 percent equity position on a commercial property. For this example, because we are investing in commercial property, we are coming out of pocket for $112,500 or 25 percent of the value of the property. The closing costs will also be significantly higher for a commercial property as compared to a residential property, but that is neither here nor there for the sake of this example.

We will assume that the property goes up in value six percent during the first year and it is now valued at $477,000. This means we generated a return of 24 percent over the first year. Our original investment was $112,500, and the property value increased by $27,000.

If we had instead invested in three single-family properties each with a value of $150,000 (total of $450,000), and instead of investing 25 percent initially we could invest 10 percent instead, our return on equity with six percent appreciation during the first year would be 60 percent. The value of the properties would increase by $27,000, and our original investment was only $45,000. By investing a smaller percentage, we are able to generate a more massive return on our equity, not only during the first year, but also for the years moving forward.

The third factor that needs to be taken into consideration is the variance in the depreciation that the IRS will allow for a commercial property versus a residential property. As we discussed previously, commercial properties are depreciated over 39 years as compared to residential properties that are depreciated over 27.5 years. This is a very significant difference. Based on a $450,000 commercial property we can depreciate in the ball park of 75 percent of the property to the tune $8,600 a year. With the three residential properties, we would have in the neighborhood of a combined depreciation of $12,272 a year, a 30 percent difference!

Now, let me make a very poignant point. Although we can see there are clearly financial benefits to holding residential properties as opposed to commercial properties, we need to understand that there is a time and a place for everything. You need to determine what the appropriate next step for you and your investing campaign is. Begin to look not only at the sheer financial rewards but also the benefits of commercial management and consistent cash flow.

There are as many different investment options as there are tenants out there. By getting together with a Real Estate Planner® you can determine the right wave for you to catch to bring your financials goals to fruition. It is critical to look at any acquisition not only for the short-term benefits but also the long-term potential. Take into account not only the management responsibilities, but also the cash flow, and how the property will allow you to maintain and grow your net worth for the years moving forward and at the same time shelter you from paying too much in taxes.

> *"Don't be afraid to take a big step if one is indicated. You can't cross a chasm in two small steps."*
>
> *David Lloyd George*

POINTS TO REMEMBER: ONE GIANT STEP – FROM INVESTMENT TO INCOME PROPERTIES

1.) You now have two primary investment options made available to you for the years moving forward. The first option is that you can perpetuate the previous growth cycle, but this time instead of acquiring one property a year for ten years, you can acquire two to four properties a year for ten years. The second alternative you have after the first 10-year period is to focus your attention on easing the management responsibilities and creating consistent cash flow as opposed to growth; this concept is the basis of this chapter.

2.) Workhorses or investment properties are structured to take advantage of massive investment returns and tax write-off opportunities.

3.) The racehorse, or income property, is a property that is very different from the workhorse. These are properties that have a very strong equity position and produce massive cash flow. They perform very well on a month-to-month basis but they don't do much to grow your wealth over an extended period of time or to minimize your tax bill.

4.) Cash flow is important; but it should not be a driving force during the early stages of wealth accumulation.

5.) On average, a thousand dollars will decrease your debt service by about $7 a month.

6.) The best way to generate cash flow is to structure your properties so that you have a strong equity position that will allow it to generate greater cash flow due to the decrease in debt service.

7.) You can either hold onto the 10 residential properties you have and allow them to generate larger and larger cash flow for the years moving forward, or you can think instead about acquiring a commercial property like an apartment building, office space, or perhaps mini-storage units with a strong equity position.

8.) Although it is possible to generate cash flow via residential income properties, there are a couple of deterrents to this strategy; they include the geographical area, the quality of tenants, and the number of tenants.

9.) There are clearly management and consistent cash flow benefits to commercial properties, but there are also tax and investment advantages to holding residential properties for income purposes.

10.) You need to determine what the appropriate next step for you and your investing campaign is. Begin to look not only at the sheer financial rewards but also the benefits of commercial management and consistent cash flow.

PART THREE

THE MONEY

FUNDING THE CAPITAL PROJECT

CHAPTER 9
TREAT YOUR HOME AS AN INVESTMENT

> *"There can be no real individual freedom in the presence of economic insecurity."*
>
> *Chester Bowles*

Everybody has heard the cliché that a house is the biggest and best investment you will ever make in your life, but not many people understand exactly the reasons *why* that statement is true *only to a point.*

The reality of this statement is that a house *is* the best investment you will ever make in your life time *if* you understand the benefits and the reasoning behind the statement.

Real estate is a tool that can be used for massive financial benefit, or it can be used simply as a place to live, which is how the majority of people and families feel about their house.

Clearly, not many people think of their home as a wealth building tool. But then again not many people 65 and older, after a lifetime of hard work, are able to support themselves without the help of their family or the government. The Social Security Administration shows that 45 percent of Americans that reach the age of 65 are still dependent on relatives, 30 percent must live on charity, and 23 percent are *still* working, perhaps they took the tortoise and the hare story to heart. Only two percent are totally independent. These numbers are absolutely staggering!

Obviously there is a connection between the choices one makes about the use of equity in their house and one's ability to one day retire independent of government or familial financial assistance. In short, there is a correct way and an incorrect way to hold financial ownership in a property.

To take a line from Stephen Covey and his book, *The 7 Habits of Highly Effective People*, put first things first. In essence, we lay the foundation first. *Your* foundation is the house that you live in. You build your wealth from this; you use this as a catapult to move you at warp speed into the world of financial independence.

The real estate planning model is to use your house as an investment, to position your equity in such a way that allows you to maximize both your return on investment and to reduce your potential tax obligation, while at the same time, still being able to comfortably make your mortgage payments so that you are not house poor.

Theoretically, the ratio of household debt to disposable income should not exceed 38 percent. What this means is that the other expenses, in addition to your mortgage payment like credit cards, car loans, and student loans, must not exceed 38 percent of your gross take home. Ideally, the amount of the bad debt, credit cards, car loans, and student loans should be minimized or eliminated, and your home loan must be maximized to meet that 38 percent ratio.

What this allows you to take advantage of are very powerful tools, leverage, and tax write-offs. Powerful appreciation, in particular, return on equity, and the tax advantages are the driving forces that make home ownership such a powerful proposition.

Unfortunately, these benefits, like a shooting star, vanish out of our sight very quickly. The longer you hold onto the original investment structure, the more you begin to grow out of the investment. And as you grow out of the investment, you quickly decrease your return on equity and you minimize your tax write-offs as you begin to pay off the loan.

RETURN ON EQUITY (ROE)

For example, let us look at how you can both botch and benefit from the powerful tool of leverage when it comes to minimizing or maximizing your return on equity for your home loan. To make a point, we will not include principal reduction in these equations. It is also important to note that these examples are based on return on equity *not* return on your original investment. The reason this is important is because you want the highest and best use of *all* of your equity, not just your original money invested.

First, how to botch leverage; if you purchase a home for $100,000 all cash, no leverage, and over the next year it increases in value six percent, you profit $6,000 and your return on your equity is a disappointing six percent. Don't get me wrong; most professional stock market investors would have mugged their own mother to get that type of return the past couple of years. But it does get much better for real estate investors.

House Value	$100,000
Financed	
Cash	$100,000
Loan	$0
House Value in 1 Year (6% appreciation)	$106,000
ROE	6%

Second, benefiting from leverage; if you purchase that same property for $100,000 but instead of paying cash, you obtain a loan for 95 percent of the house or $95,000, you only use $5,000 of your own money. Again, over the next year, the home appreciates six percent in value to $106,000. But this time your return on your equity is a massive 120 percent rather than six percent because your original investment was $5,000 not $100,000. Clearly, all else being equal, a 120 percent return is much better than a six percent return.

House Value	$100,000
Financed	
Cash	$5,000
Loan	$95,000
House Value in 1 Year (6% appreciation)	$106,000
ROE	120%

The caveat that disrupts this return on equity is the application of time. Again, we will look at this same example but we will put it out five years from now and look at the return on equity on the 5th year; the annual appreciation will remain at six percent.

House Value	$100,000
Financed	
Cash	$100,000
Loan	$0
House Value in 4th Year	$126,247
House Value in 5th Year (6% appreciation)	$133,822
ROE 5th Year	$7575/$133,822 = 5.7%

In this example, the return on equity decreased slightly due to the compounding effect of this type of investment. However, there is not a meaningful or significant change compared to what you will see in the next example.

House Value	\$100,000
Financed	
Cash	\$5,000
Loan	\$95,000
House Value in 4th Year	\$126,247
House Value in 5th Year	\$133,822
(6% appreciation)	
ROE 5th Year	\$7575/\$38822 = 19.5%

So in five years, the property that *was* highly leveraged and produced a return on equity of 120 percent in the first year, now in the 5th year is producing a return on equity of 19.5 percent. Clearly, the downward trend for this return will continue unless the financing for the property is restructured so as to reflect a decrease in equity position or increased loan to value ratio. In Exhibit 3 in the Appendix, there is a chart that illustrates the massive power that comes with having a highly leveraged or low equity position property. Again this chart illustrates return on equity, *not* return on your original investment. The equity position is determined by dividing your equity into the value of the property.

The goal during the growth stage is to maintain a minimum of a 30 percent return on equity position on your primary residence. Clearly, the frequency for the need to refinance your house is contingent upon the annual appreciation percentage. The higher the annual appreciation, the quicker you can refinance or sell the property to get your equity out and put that money to work. The slower the annual appreciation, the longer it will take before you can take the equity out of your residence.

RETURN ON INVESTMENT (ROI)

Return on Investment is another effective equation that can be used to see your return on your *original* investment. This type of analysis is important because it allows you to compare apples to apples with other types of investment vehicles like insurance, equities or stocks, and CD's, or bonds. We will take a look at these comparisons in Chapter 14 when we "make the case" for this framework.

Return on Investment is different from Return on Equity in that ROI will increase the longer you have the property while ROE will decrease the longer you have the property. The reason for this is simple; your *investment* is the money you *originally* put down on the property. It is a one-time investment. Return on Equity is an ever-changing equation because your equity is always increasing in the property. Your equity increases in one of two ways, either via principal reduction or through appreciation of the property.

Often times money managers will calculate the time it takes for an investment to double in value. This determinant is based off of the return on investment. To determine how soon it will take for your property to double in value simply take 72 and divide it by the annual appreciation (Exhibit 5: The Rule of "72"). For example, if the appreciation percentage is six percent, it will take 12 years for your property to double in value. If the annual appreciation is 12 percent, it will take only six years for your property to double in value.

YOUR LARGEST ANNUAL BILL – YOUR TAX BILL

So we have examined how to both botch and benefit from the use of leverage in terms of return on equity. Now lets look at the flip side of the coin, the tax implications of a property that is free and clear of any loans verses one that is highly leveraged.

With a house that you own free and clear, your only tax deduction is the property taxes. On the other hand, by having a mortgage the IRS allows you to write off the interest you pay on your primary residence. This concept is directly related to the previous example in that the less your equity position, or the more highly leveraged your property is, the more interest you will pay on your loan and thus the greater your tax write-off will be. Clearly it makes sense that you should take advantage of this write-off. This write-off hits your bottom line in addition to the property taxes you pay.

THE BIG PICTURE

By leveraging your property, you can maximize both your return on equity as well as your tax write-off opportunities. So the big picture is this; not only should you maximize your return on equity and your tax deductions when you acquire a property, but you must also manage your return on equity and your tax write-off opportunities in your property as the house appreciates over time.

An easy way to manage these two variables is to keep up to date with a comparative market analysis or CMA, and to review the ratio of your equity against the value of your house. Just as a stockholder researches, evaluates, and makes decisions based on the value of shares he or she owns, you too will research, evaluate, and make decisions based on the value of your house. Once your property grows into a 20 percent equity to 80 percent loan ratio, you should think about selling, refinancing, or getting a line of credit against your house to get your equity out. Of course if you are going to sell your house, it must not only support the cost of sale, but there must be a significant amount of equity or financial reasoning to make that type of a move. The Inside the Box Acquisition Model would support this type of scenario. If you were to merely refinance the property in a six percent appreciation market this type of transaction could take place every three to four years. In addition the action of refinancing and getting your equity out would allow you to use your equity to acquire other rental properties.

You might be thinking that, "if I keep refinancing it is going to cost me money and I will never get this house paid off," and you would be correct for thinking this. Our goal, your goal during the wealth building stage is *not* to get your house paid off but rather to do two things, maximize your return on equity (highest and best use) and to minimize your potential tax obligation; that is it.

Two warnings, when it comes to loans, first, *never* obtain a new loan with a pre-payment penalty. There are plenty of good loans and companies that do not have these clauses. Second, PMI or Private Mortgage Insurance can and should be avoided when obtaining a new loan, and in most instances, you don't need 20 percent equity to avoid it.

The rule for PMI is that a loan can not exceed 80 percent of the value of the property or you will have to obtain mortgage insurance which is *not* a tax write-off on primary residences. The way around this is to have a first loan for 80 percent and a second loan for 20, 15, 10, or even 5 percent of the balance depending on your equity position. The second mortgage traditionally will have a higher interest rate and thus will lend itself to more of a tax write-off at the end of the year. Fortunately, this fits right in with our goal to maximize our return on equity and to minimize our potential tax obligation.

This, after all, is how you win the game and become financially independent. You maximize your return on investments and you create tax shelters so that on paper you minimize or eliminate any of those massive gains that you have experienced.

So now you have your foundation for financial independence and abundance established. You have a highly leveraged property generating a minimum of at least a 30 percent annual return on equity for you; you can still pay your mortgage because your household debt does not exceed 38 percent of your gross income, and you are maximizing your tax write-offs through the interest and the property taxes you pay on your primary residence. You must accomplish and manage these objectives before you can begin to build and grow your real estate empire.

If you are not currently on this path, either you switch lanes and get on the fast track to financial independence and you be part of the two percent of Americans aged 65 and older who are financially independent, or you can continue to do what you have been doing and you can stay with the 98 percent of the American population that just don't get it.

> *"If your money is not working hard for you, then you will have to start working hard for your money."*
>
> *Mark P. Mac Kenzie*

POINTS TO REMEMBER: TREAT YOUR HOME AS AN INVESTMENT

1.) A house *is* the best investment you will ever make in your life time *if* you understand the benefits and the reasoning behind the statement.

2.) The Social Security Administration shows that 45 percent of Americans that reach the age of 65 are still dependent on relatives, 30 percent must live on charity, and 23 percent are *still* working. Only two percent are financially independent.

3.) The real estate planning model is to use your house as an investment, to position your equity in such a way that allows you to maximize both your return on investment and to reduce your potential tax obligation while at the same time still being able to comfortably make your mortgage payments, so that you are not house poor.

4.) The longer you hold onto the original investment structure, the more you begin to grow out of the investment. And as you grow out of the investment, you quickly decrease your return on equity and you minimize your tax write-offs as you begin to payoff the loan.

5.) An easy way to manage your return on equity is to keep up-to-date with a comparative market analysis, and to review the ratio of your equity against the value of your property. Once your house grows into a 20 percent equity to 80 percent loan ratio, you should think about selling, refinancing, or getting a line of credit against your property to get your equity out.

CHAPTER 10
YOUR EQUITY, YOUR MONEY, AND YOUR CREDIT CARDS

"If you can count your money, you don't have a billion dollars."

J. Paul Getty

YOUR EQUITY

Now that we have laid the foundation with how to manage the equity in your house so as to maximize your return on equity and your tax write-offs, we are going to look at ways to not only access your equity but also explain systems for saving money as well as using credit cards for shoestring investors.

There are five ways to tap into the equity in your property and each of them has a purpose. You can sell the house, hold a mortgage, refinance to get money out tax free, get a 2nd mortgage, or you can get a line of credit against your equity.

First, selling your property has a benefit because you are able to get *all* of your equity out. The downside is that it costs money to sell your house; these costs are in the form of commissions and closing fees; it takes time, and there may be tax consequences depending on how long you have owned the property or what the property was used for.

Second, holding a mortgage has massive benefits because you are able to make a powerful gain on your equity due to the interest that you charge on the mortgage that you hold.

The downside is that clearly it takes time to get your equity back and there are also tax consequences.

Third, refinancing allows you to get most, if not all, of your equity out tax-free and within a reasonable time period of 30-45 days. The downside is that you do have closing costs when you obtain the new loan.

Fourth, a 2nd mortgage allows you to tap into most, if not all, of your equity tax-free. The 2nd gives you this equity in a lump sum. The cost and benefit of a 2nd mortgage is that it does charge you interest to get at your equity, but the interest that you pay is tax deductible just as the interest is on your 1st mortgage.

Fifth, a line of credit also allows you to tap into most, if not all, of your equity tax-free. The line of credit is more flexible than a 2nd; it allows you to draw on various amounts as opposed to a lump sum of your equity; it provides much more latitude. The cost and the benefit of a line of credit is that it does cost you interest to get at your line of credit, but the interest that you pay is tax deductible, just as the interest is on your 1st mortgage.

The important thing to remember is that your equity is intended to be used to grow your wealth in the highest and best manner possible. The methods explained in this chapter are the most expeditious ways to be successful with the investing framework.

YOUR MONEY

> *"Happiness lies not in the mere possession of money. It lies in the joy of achievement, in the thrill of creative effort."*
>
> *Franklin Delano Roosevelt*

The emphasis of this chapter is clearly intended to educate you on how to release and liquidate your equity in your property or properties so as to maximize your return on equity and your tax write-offs. In essence, the intent of this investing campaign is to be able to accomplish the framework in a self-perpetuating fashion. In short, it should not be necessary to continually "come-out-of-pocket" to make this framework successful for you.

The reality of investing in real estate is that there may be times when you *do* want to use your money as opposed to your equity to acquire properties. This may be because you want to put more significant down-payments on properties or you want to acquire more than one property a year. If this is your intent, then you have another option, the old-fashioned way, you save it. You can literally begin funneling money from your work paycheck into an additional cash reserve account.

Let's assume you are following the Straight Line-Acquisition Model. You are going to turn your house into a rental and you are going to acquire another property that you will move into as your primary residence. The effective way to do this is to determine how much money you need to save based on the down-payment and closing costs and to work backwards from there. So, if you are going to acquire a $150,000 property with an FHA loan, you will need to invest at least three percent for a down-payment. You may also decide that you don't want to pay closing costs so you are going to wrap those fees into the loan amount.

This means that you need to save $4,500 over the next 12 months to acquire the property. This equates to $375 a month you would need to save for the next 12 months. This may or may not seem like a lot of money to some people. If it does seem like a lot of money, consider that it is prudent to keep 15 percent of all that you make. This means that $375 is 15 percent of $2,500 a month. If you make $2,500 a month, you make $30,000 a year.

According to the U.S. Census Bureau the *median* household income in 2001 was $42,228.

What do all of these numbers mean? It is very simple, unless you are making less than $30,000 a year, which is close to 30 percent below the national median for household income, and you are reckless with your money, there is no reason why you can't work this investing framework and retire in 10 years. *You don't have to be rich, or well-off to buy properties, you have to be smart.*

YOUR CREDIT CARDS

Credit cards have received a bad rap over the past two decades, and for good reason. In most instances credit cards are abused and are used almost exclusively to acquire depreciating assets or consumer items like entertainment systems, clothes, or even vacations. None of these purchases get you any closer to being financially independent.

The benefit of credit cards is that they can be a good source of quick cash in emergency situations. For a real estate investor, emergency situations may include expensive repairs or extended vacancies for your properties. In a perfect world each property that you own will have a three-month mortgage reserve to go with it. In reality, things happen, and sometimes that reserve may not be there. If you are investing on a shoe-string budget, credit cards may be a good safeguard for the short term. Keep in mind, this is for emergency purposes only; credit cards or cash advances should *not* be used to acquire properties.

One last caveat on credit cards, they will only be as effective as your credit is good. If you have good credit you can begin to grow your cash advance and credit limits. This will come in handy when you have 10 properties on the books. If your credit has some spots on it, begin trying to rebuild it, start showing that credit companies can trust you and start paying your bills on time. Otherwise, they may not be there when you need them to be.

> *"Save a little money each month and at the end of the year you'll be surprised at how little you have."*
>
> *Ernest Haskins*

POINTS TO REMEMBER: YOUR EQUITY, YOUR MONEY, AND YOUR CREDIT CARDS

1.) There are five ways to tap into the equity in your property and each of them has a cost and benefit. You can sell the house, hold a mortgage, refinance to get money out tax free, get a 2nd mortgage, or you can get a line of credit against your equity.

2.) The reality of investing in real estate is that there may be times when you do want to use your money as opposed to your equity to acquire properties. The best way to do this is through a monthly savings or cash management account.

3.) Credit cards are the third source for funding the framework. The benefit of credit cards is that they can be a good source of quick cash in emergency situations.

CHAPTER 11
OTHER PEOPLE'S MONEY

"Lack of money is no obstacle. Lack of an idea is an obstacle."

Ken Hakuta

The great advantage to investing in real estate is that you don't need to use a significant amount of your money to acquire an enormous asset. In fact, in some instances, even traditional ones, you don't need to use *any* of *your* money to acquire an asset. The investment in real estate is an investment that is able to be secured by the asset or property itself. Because the investment can be secured, lending institutions or private individual lenders are more than willing to lend you money, in some cases, all the money necessary to acquire the property.

The consensus amongst intelligent investors and financially savvy individuals is that if you don't have to use any of your own money, don't. This includes down-payments and closing costs. On average, for every $1,000 you amortize into a loan, it will cost you an extra $7 a month. So instead of paying $5,000 in closing costs, it may be more financially prudent to roll or amortize the closing costs into the loan and increase your payments by $35 a month. With this strategy, it would take over 142 months or close to 12 years for you to "pay off that part of the loan;" this is a good thing. This strategy keeps you liquid or able to acquire more properties with money that would have otherwise been used to pay for closing costs.

This chapter will discuss other tips and tricks to using other people's money, both traditional and untraditional methods. As you may have already guessed, each of these financing techniques and strategies have their costs and benefits, and it will depend on the situation to determine which one will work best for you. The reality is that these tools give you latitude when acquiring properties. The bottom line is that it does not matter so much how or where you acquire properties, just that you do acquire them. This chapter will cover Conventional, Interest-only, FHA, and VA loans, the dreaded Private Mortgage Insurance, as well as cash purchases and seller financing. This book is not a book on loans; so if you need more information, web site addresses have been provided for you.

One word of caution before we jump into loans; it was mentioned in a previous chapter, but I will mention it again because it is very significant, beware of pre-payment penalties with loans. There are far too many brokers and bankers out there to have to settle for a loan with a pre-payment penalty. Do not invest in a loan that has one of these; it significantly limits your flexibility with your future financing decisions.

CONVENTIONAL FINANCING

Conventional financing allows you to take advantage of a number of financing options. Conventional programs allow you unlimited loan limits and favorable interest rates. Conventional loans are divided into ARMs or Adjustable Rate Mortgages and fixed rate loans, both of which have various types of terms. There is no limit to a conventional loan although anything larger than a jumbo loan ($322,700) will carry with it a higher interest rate. In regards to interest rates, conventional loans provide a wide variety of programs that are contingent upon the type of loan program. And of course, different loan programs require different down-payments.

ARMs have several features that will vary from product to product. These features include the initial rate, how often that rate or payment will change, the index with which the rate will change, the margin that is added to the index, and the cap both on the adjustment period and over the life of the loan, that the interest rate can rise or fall.

The 5/1 and 3/1 are the most common types of ARMs. These numbers mean that the rate will be fixed for the first five or three years respectively, at a lower rate, and then will adjust every year there after. The reason why these are so popular is because many people will not stay in a property for anymore than three to five years.

Interest rates with ARMs are more favorable than that of fixed-term loans. They can usually be a point to a point and a half lower than that of a 30-year or 15-year fixed loan. The cost of moving forward with an ARM is the unknown variable that may make these loans a bit tricky to manage. In the short-term the rate is favorable, but long-term you don't know what direction the rates are heading. The ARM is a good tool to use for an IRC 121 property acquisition.

Fixed rates are just that, fixed. The most common types of fixed rate loans are 30 and 15-year loans. As mentioned previously, these may be a point to a point and a half higher than that of an ARM. But clearly, they do have their benefits, the most profound one being that the rate is locked, so you know that 10 years from now your payment will remain the same. The 15-year fixed carries a lower interest rate than the 30-year, usually about a half point. The benefit of doing a 15-year loan is that you pay the loan off quicker and you pay less interest over the life of the loan. The cost of doing a 15-year loan is that you pay the loan off quicker and you pay less interest over the life of the loan which results in less tax write-offs over the 15-year period. It is a double-edged sword. And as you remember, your goal is to increase your return on equity and to reduce your potential tax obligation during the growth stage of your investing campaign. The 15-year fixed loan may be a good idea during the passive cash flow stage of your investing.

There are a variety of down-payment options and programs available with conventional financing. Loans can be funded with as little as zero percent down if your credit willing, or with as much as you want to put down. Of most importance if you are putting down less than 20 percent equity, is to be sure that your first loan or mortgage does not exceed 80 percent. The reason this is important is because a loan with greater than 80 percent will require mortgage insurance, commonly referred to as private mortgage insurance (PMI) or mortgage insurance premium (MIP). The alternative is to get a second loan for 20, 15, 10, or even 5 percent of the loan. What this allows you to do is to maximize your leverage or return on equity, your tax write-offs, and not pay any mortgage insurance which is not a tax write-off on your primary residence. Mortgage insurance is a junk cost and should be avoided when possible.

INTEREST-ONLY LOANS

Another type of conventional loan that was more popular in the 1920's and is making a big comeback the past couple of years, is the interest-only loan. The way this type of loan works is the borrower pays only the interest on the loan for a predetermined period of time. The predetermined period of time can be anywhere from a couple of years to up to 10 years in some instances. At the end of this period, the amortization will take place over the remaining balance of the loan. These types of loans are commonly ARMs.

For example, an interest-only loan could be a 30-year term loan with the first 10 years being interest-only payments. If the loan amount were $100,000 at an interest rate of 6.5 percent, instead of the monthly payment being $629 with principal and interest, the payment would be $542 of interest-only. These payments would be paid over the term of the interest-only period and then the loan balance would be amortized over the remaining 20 years. The payments over the remaining 20 years would then increase to $746 a month from the $542 to include the addition of the principal payments. More than likely, the loan will be paid off before this would happen as this framework does not have any purpose for holding a property for longer than a 10-year period.

The interest-only loan has many benefits including smaller payments, more tax write-offs, an improved ROE over the 10-year term, as well as the ability to acquire a larger asset. In fact, there is really very little drawback to these types of loans. A consideration though is that the lower the interest rate, the more advantageous these loans will be.

For example, at 3.5 percent interest, the monthly payment would be reduced by 35 percent. At 6.5 percent interest, the monthly payment would be reduced by 14 percent. At 9.5 percent interest, the monthly payment decreases by 5 percent. And at 12.5 percent interest, the monthly payment barely reduces by 1.5 percent. Stated simply, the lower the interest rate for the loan, the less interest you pay every month. Interest-only loans are most effective when you are not paying much in interest.

Interest-only loans are a very powerful tool that allows the borrower to increase the return on equity as well as to maximize tax deductions.

In summary, conventional financing provides buyers with many acquisition strategies. The only caveat is that it is true to name; it is conventional, and there may be extenuating circumstances that for one reason or another you will not be able to use this type of financing. Examples of these types of opportunities include quick closes of a week or 10 days, a buyer that is not able to qualify for a conventional program, or even a property that you cannot get hazard insurance for.

The explanation for the hazard insurance is that every loan requires you to have insurance on the property, but wisely so; insurance companies are very specific with the type of properties they will insure, and they are unlikely to insure vacant, abandoned, or severely distressed and run down properties.

The safest way to protect yourself from this pitfall is to have your insurance agent pull up a CLUE (Comprehensive Loss and Underwriting Exchange) report on the house or property before you commit to purchasing it. The CLUE report will tell you if the property has had any past claims against it and whether or not it is insurable for starters, and whether or not you will have to pay a premium if it is in fact insurable. Generally speaking, the more claims that have been made with a property, the more difficult it will be to insure.

FHA FINANCING

The FHA or the Federal Housing Administration, to a point, is another good source for financing your acquisitions. The FHA guidelines are very straight forward in regards to loan limit. They will vary county to county but are in the range of the $150,000's. The term is a 30-year fixed and the interest rate will usually fall a half point above a conventional fixed loan. For more information on FHA loans go to:

www.hud.gov

The loan limit may or may not be an obstacle for you depending on the value of the property you are acquiring. This type of loan is perfect for a buy and hold strategy if you plan on moving into the property you are acquiring and at a later date turning that property into a rental.

The underwriting process is very simple; make your payments on time for 12 months, and chances are you can qualify for the loan. Traditionally, FHA requires three percent down, which, relatively speaking, is powerful because most conventional loans require at least five percent down. However, what has been taking place over the past few years has been the emergence of gift foundations like AmeriDream, CDS home grants, and Home Grants USA.

What these programs allow the buyer to do is to have up to 10 percent of their closing costs and down-payment gifted by the seller to a third party intermediary, AmeriDream, Home Grants USA, or CDS Home Grants, and then onto the buyer. The charge for this is anywhere from $350 to ¾ of a point.

The reality of this gift is that the sum gifted more often than not is wrapped into the loan. So the buyer still pays handsomely over the life of the loan for the gift, but it does enable him or her to acquire the property for nothing down and again maximizing the return on equity and tax write-off opportunities.

To find our more information on these types of programs go to:

www.AmeriDream.org
www.HomeGrantsUSA.org

You can determine which assistance program will work best for your needs. For now, understand that these programs are available to you. These gift programs can be used in conjunction with conventional loans as well. The reason they are placed under the FHA umbrella is that they are most commonly used with FHA loans.

VETERAN'S ADMINISTRATION FINANCING

The VA is a great source of funds for veterans. These loans allow veterans to acquire a property, no money down, with no mortgage insurance, and flexible qualifying conditions. To find out more on this type of loan go take a look at their web site listed below.

www.homeloans.va.gov/veteran.htm

PRIVATE MORTGAGE INSURANCE (PMI)

PMI is a very misunderstood concept. PMI only comes into play with FHA mortgages and more specifically with conventional 1st loans that exceed greater than 80 percent loan to value. So with a conventional loan if you only put down 10 percent and you get a 1st loan for 90 percent, you will pay PMI. However, if you are smart, and you will be after reading this book, you can find ways around paying PMI.

Pay attention here; you can have a conventional acquisition with a 1st loan at 80 percent and a 2nd loan at 20 percent and *not* pay mortgage insurance because the 1st loan does not exceed 80 percent, no money down conventional loan, no PMI, it is true. Basically, there are a couple of "piggyback" loans that allow you to sidestep the PMI while at the same time you don't have to put down 20 percent. These loans are the 80-5-15, 80-10-10, 80-15-5, 80-20-0. The first number is the 1st loan, the second number is the 2nd loan, and the third number is your down-payment.

The drawback to PMI is that it is not tax deductible on your primary residence like mortgage interest is. PMI is however tax deductible on an income or investment property because it is a cost of business.

The bottom line is that PMI should not be a *major* concern when deciding how to acquire a property. The reality is that the returns you will receive on your investment will far outweigh the added cost of supporting the PMI. Trying to avoid paying PMI is something you should do; avoiding investing *because* of PMI is a colossal mistake.

CASH FINANCING

Cash financing has several benefits. It takes less time, there are very little closing costs involved, the loan costs are eliminated, you are not required to obtain hazard insurance, and obviously you don't need to qualify for a loan or have one show up on your credit report and effect your debt to income ratio for future loans.

The greatest benefit for cash financing is time, or perhaps more appropriately, the lack of time it takes to acquire and close on a property. Cash acquisitions provide a powerful opportunity to close on a property in 3-10 days with the only contingency being the title company. The significance this time variable has is completely dependent on the seller. For some sellers, time is not a factor; their first priority is their net. But for other sellers facing foreclosure, divorced couples, or other distressed property owners, time is priceless. And because of the price they put on the commodity of time, they will pay.

The most effective way to use this tool of cash financing is to leverage the acquisition based on time, and then once the property is acquired and off of the seller's hands, go ahead and refinance with more conventional methods. Cash financing should not be an end all for the transaction. By holding a property in full cash, you have wiped clean any significant return on equity and any resemblance of a tax write-off.

SELLER-FINANCING

Seller-financing or seller carry-backs have a multitude of benefits, the most significant one being that *everything* is negotiable. Where as conventional and FHA financing have underwriting guidelines, time requirements for loan documents, appraisals that need to be met, origination fees and charges, down-payment requirements, and interest rate minimums, seller carry-backs do not have these restrictions. Also of note, clearly any loan that you have that is carried by a seller will not show up on your credit report. What this equates to, more often than not, is a more favorable credit rating than if you had the loan through a traditional lending institution. Your debt to income ratio will not be negatively impacted.

Seller carry-backs do not have qualifying guidelines; the acquisition can happen with a much shorter timetable, and it costs less to close with this type of a loan as opposed to a more traditional lending source.

A very common financing stipulation with seller carry-backs are balloon payments. Balloon payments are also found in traditional financing as well, but as you will learn, are understandably much more common with seller carry-backs. Balloon payments are a clause in the loan that state when the principal balance of the loan is due and payable. A very common example of this is for the seller to carry the note with a 30-year amortization but to have the payoff or balloon due in 5, 10 or 15 years. In short, this means that the buyer would need to get a new traditional loan to pay off the seller in this time period.

In some rare instances, the seller will carry the note for the entire 30 or 15-year term, but more commonly, the seller does want to get his or her equity out and do something else with the money. Perhaps if the terms are so favorable for the seller, this won't be the case, but hopefully and especially after reading this book, you will be wise enough to get *your* terms on the note, not the seller's.

Favorable terms for a buyer for a seller carry-back would be a no or low money down situation with an interest rate par or sub par to that of the going traditional rate. Although it may be tough to have your cake and eat it too, more often than not, it would be in your best interest to put down as little money as possible so as to maximize your return on equity. If this means paying a point or two higher than the market par rate, it may very well be worth it. However, you must be certain to run the numbers to make sure the property will still cash flow as you need it to do so.

"Finance is the art of passing money from hand to hand until it finally disappears."

Robert W. Sarnoff

POINTS TO REMEMBER: OTHER PEOPLE'S MONEY

1.) The great advantage to investing in real estate is that you don't need to use a significant amount of your money to acquire an enormous asset.

2.) Beware of pre-payment penalties with loans. There are far too many brokers and bankers out there to have to settle for a loan with a pre-payment penalty.

3.) Conventional financing allows you to take advantage of a number of financing options. Conventional programs allow you unlimited loan limits and favorable interest rates.

4.) Interest-only loans allow the borrower to pay only the interest on the loan for a predetermined period of time. In some instances this will allow for reductions in monthly payments of over 15 percent.

5.) FHA loans have more rigid loan limits, less latitude with underwriting, and higher interest rates. They are, however, great loans to assist people to buy properties that would not be able to under Conventional guidelines.

6.) Veterans Administration loans allow veterans to acquire a property, no money down, with no mortgage insurance, and flexible qualifying conditions.

7.) Private Mortgage Insurance only comes into play with FHA mortgages and more specifically with Conventional 1st loans that exceed greater than 80 percent loan to value.

8.) Cash financing has several benefits. It takes less time, there are very little closing costs involved, the loan costs are eliminated, you are not required to obtain hazard insurance, and obviously you don't need to qualify for a loan or have one show up on your credit report and effect your debt to income ratio for future loans.

9.) Seller financing or seller carry-backs have a multitude of benefits, the most significant one being that *everything* is negotiable.

CHAPTER 12
USING THE IRS

"To be conscious that you are ignorant is a great step to knowledge."

Benjamin Disraeli

WHAT YOU THOUGHT YOU KNEW, BUT DIDN'T KNOW

"Poverty has many roots, but the taproot is ignorance."

Lyndon B. Johnson

What is the largest expense Americans have every year, their mortgage, credit cards, health insurance? How about their tax bill; most people don't think about taxes as an expense, but it is. The harsh reality for most people is that their tax bill is larger than their housing, food, and clothing bill, *combined.* It is about time you begin to start thinking in this light because if you're not, you are *losing* money. Real Estate is the only investment, other than owning a business, that allows you to decrease your largest expense, your tax bill.

Real Estate is directly wired into the tax codes. It is the only investment medium that has a multitude of tax advantages. What this means to you, the investor, is that you have many tools to choose from when making investment decisions.

Despite some changes that have taken place within the IRS that have eradicated some of the tax shelters that real estate investors have benefited from in the past, the IRS still provides many incentives to individuals that wisely choose to invest in real estate. These benefits include specific revenue codes, depreciation opportunities, and refinancing loop holes.

The two IRS codes that have provided profound benefits to real estate owners and investors are IRC 121 and IRC 1031.

IRC 121

First, the Taxpayer Relief Act of 1997 or IRC 121 provides homeowners and investors with a very powerful tax law. IRC 121 stated very simply, allows single filers or joint filers, a $250,000 or $500,000 respectively, tax-free exemption in regards to capital gains on the sale of a primary residence if they have owned *and* lived in the property for two out of the last five years.

What this means is that an individual or married couple may live in a primary residence for two out of five years and realize a gain of up to and not in excess of $250,000 or $500,000 tax-free, no strings attached.

The benefits of this code have two general applications. First, it clearly allows for individuals or married couples to move from their primary residence every two years and realize a significant amount of capital gain tax-free. Second, it allows investors, if their lifestyle permits, to move in to one of their investment properties for two years and then sell the property without paying any taxes for capital gains. (Of course with this second strategy, the property owner would still be responsible for depreciation recapture taxes.)

The first strategy lends itself to a pre-meditated investment campaign of moving your household every two years. This would allow the individual or couple a very significant amount of tax-free gain over a period of six to eight years or three to four moves. The one caveat is that the selection of the property must lend itself to achieving a sizeable or significant gain.

There are three ways to stack the odds in your favor for being able to realize this significant capital gain in an *average* real estate market. First, you can acquire a house wholesale from the tertiary market. Second, you can acquire a house in a new subdivision and anticipate higher than average appreciation points the first year or two. Or three, you can build a house. This would obviously allow you to buy or build at cost.

In a bull, or above average real estate market, the chances are very good that you will be able to move into any house at cost or retail and in two years experience a significant gain so as to have the same effect as mentioned previously. Unfortunately, with this type of example, geography plays a significant factor and thus leaves us without any options other than to move to New England or California. For example, Rhode Island experienced approximately a 16 percent increase in housing prices over the past year. Arizona, where I live, on the other hand experienced just a little over 5.5 percent appreciation in property values the past year.

The second application of IRC 121 is for real estate investors, in particular those that buy and hold single family properties. Before IRC 121 came into being in 1997, investors had limited options when selling an investment property they had owned. They could carry a mortgage, do a 1031 exchange, or sell the property outright and pay capital gain taxes and depreciation recapture. What 121 allows investors to do is to move into an investment property for two years and then sell the property and not pay capital gains taxes. The investor would still be responsible for depreciation recapture, but clearly the tax consequences would be significantly reduced.

IRC 1031

IRC 1031, sometimes referred to as a tax "free" exchange, like-kind exchange, or Starker Exchange, but more appropriately referred to as a tax "deferred" exchange, allows investors to trade up in property value while not having to immediately pay capital gains taxes or depreciation recapture. In short, the investor can acquire a larger asset on the back half of the exchange than he or she would have been able to acquire had he or she not performed a 1031 exchange.

Of course with these types of benefits, the IRS has also developed some clear guidelines for performing a qualified and approved 1031 exchange.

The rules are fairly simple. First, when performing an exchange you must acquire a property or properties that are of equal to or greater value than the relinquished property. Second, the exchange funds must be transferred through a qualified intermediary. The seller of the property cannot have contact with the funds once his or her property has been sold. Third, the seller has 45 days to name the new property or properties and 180 days to close on it or them. If any of these rules are violated the exchange will be ruled out.

Although the benefits of shielding the tax consequences of the sale of an investment property are massive, it is first important to know where we stand in regards to the adjusted basis so that we know what our gain in the property is going to be.

To determine the capital gain that you will be responsible for upon the sale of your property you need to first calculate the adjusted basis. The adjusted basis is very simply:

ADJUSTED BASIS

Original Purchase Price + Purchase Expenses + Capital Improvements - Depreciation Taken = Adjusted Basis

Once we have the adjusted basis we can then subtract this number as well as the selling expenses from the sales price of the property to determine the capital gain.

CAPITAL GAIN

Sales Price - Selling Expenses - Adjusted Basis = Capital Gain

You should always consult with an accountant in determining what your adjusted basis is and what your capital gain will be.

Once we know what the capital gain is, we can then begin to make an educated decision as to whether or not we should move forward with a 1031 exchange.

Let us take a look at a hypothetical example and see how the benefits of a 1031 exchange unfold for an owner.

We will assume that the seller has a property valued at $500,000 and that the seller bought the property for

$250,000. There is $250,000 of debt and the property has been fully depreciated. This means that the seller will be responsible for the depreciation recapture taxes on $187,500 (amount depreciated over 39 years) and the taxes on the $250,000 of capital gain if he or she does not perform a 1031 exchange. The following would be an *example* of the consequences at the federal and state level if a 1031 exchange is not performed.

Federal
Depreciation Recapture
$187,500 x 25% = $46,875

Capital Gain Balance
$250,000 x 20% = $50,000

Federal Taxes Owed
$96,875

State (AZ)
State Taxes Owed
$437,500 x 3.74% = $16,362

Total State and Federal Taxes Owed
$113,237

Capital gains are taxed at 20 percent by the Fed and will also incur an additional fractional tax on the state level. This amount will vary from state to state. For this example we used Arizona at 3.74 percent. Arizona has one of the lower capital gains rates in the country. Just to give you an example, California comes in at 9 percent and Montana tops the charts at 10 percent for capital gains tax rates.

Now that we understand the consequences, we will take a look at how these consequences affect the acquisition of the new property or properties on the back side of the 1031 exchange.

Sale
Equity $250,000
Capital Gain Tax $113,237
Cash to Reinvest $136,763

New Property
(Assuming 75% Loan to Value)
$547,052

Exchange
Equity $250,000
Capital Gain Tax $0
Cash to Reinvest $250,000

New Property
(Assuming 75% Loan to Value)
$1,000,000

Although this is just one example, it illustrates a powerful opportunity of not only how to save money in taxes but also how to increase the purchasing power when acquiring another property or properties. *On a side note, for the love of all that is good in this world, start the exchange process **before** you close on the relinquished property.*

DEPRECIATION

Depreciation is a powerful tax write-off tool that applies exclusively to investment or income properties rather than to owner-occupied properties.

There are two different types of depreciation. One type applies to residential properties and the other to commercial properties.

The concept of depreciation is that the property, more specifically the actual building or structure, will be used and worn, and that after a certain period of time, it will no longer be functional or able to be used for the desired effect.

An important note to be aware of is that you can only depreciate the building or improved structure; you cannot depreciate the land. A fairly conservative estimate is to give the land 25 percent of the value of the entire property. So if you have a $100,000 property, you can depreciate $75,000. The remaining $25,000 is the value of the land.

The first type of depreciation, the type that applies to residential properties, is taken over 27.5 years. This means that on the $100,000 property, we can depreciate the $75,000 over 27.5 years. This would generate $2,727 in an annual tax write-off.

The second type of depreciation, the type that applies to commercial properties, is taken over 39 years. This means that on the $100,000 property, we can depreciate the $75,000 over 39 years. This would generate $1,923 in an annual tax write-off.

Clearly the benefits are far greater for depreciating residential rather than commercial properties, but both provide a consistent tax break to investors.

Although depreciation is a powerful opportunity while holding a property, it also can be a devastating hindrance when selling because it needs to be “recaptured” if you do not perform a 1031 exchange. The Fed will tax this “gain” at a 25 percent clip. Always have an accountant help you determine the tax consequences and “costs” before selling your property outright.

REFINANCE

"Refinancing is God's gift to Real Estate Investors."

Mark P. Mac Kenzie

Refinancing in some respects is the most powerful tool that an investor has. It is quick, cost efficient, and tax-free.

It is quick in that most refinances will take no longer than 30 days. Relatively speaking, this tool makes real estate fairly liquid as compared to the time it will take you to *sell* the property. Depending on the property, if it is priced properly, it may take 60-90 days to get an offer and another 30-45 days to close. Refinancing can significantly reduce this window of time.

The cost-effectiveness of refinancing is also relative compared to the alternative to selling the property. The only fees you have with refinancing are the lender fees; where as with a sale you will incur real estate sales commissions and escrow or title fees instead of just the lending fees.

Most importantly, refinancing and getting a cash-out loan on your property is not a taxable transaction. For the gain to be taxable, you need to sell the property.

An important point to note is that although you can extract some of your equity from the property tax free via a refinance, this does not alleviate you from paying capital gain and depreciation-recapture taxes when you sell the property. In essence, the refinance is a temporary band-aid that allows you to get at your equity tax-free.

An important note on refinancing is that you still need to qualify for the new loan. The reason this may be an obstacle is that when you do a cash-out loan, you are at the same time adjusting your debt to income ratios. By getting cash out, you are obtaining a new and larger loan, this means more debt service. If you cannot support the desired ratios, you will not be able to pull the money out. This is why it benefits you to stay conservative when it comes to your debt to income ratios. It provides you more latitude to negotiate financing decisions.

> *"The only difference between death and taxes is that death doesn't get worse every time Congress meets."*
>
> *Will Rogers*

POINTS TO REMEMBER: USING THE IRS

1.) The IRS will be your greatest ally on your journey to accumulating massive amounts of wealth.

2.) The IRC 121 allows homeowners to sell a house every two years for a tax free capital gain of $250,000 for single filers or $500,000 for joint filers as long as they have lived in and owned the property for two out of five years.

3.) IRC 1031 allows for a tax deferred exchange in which investors can sell investment properties without having to pay taxes on capital gain or depreciation recapture as long as they acquire a property or properties during a specific window of time that are equal to or greater in value than the relinquished property.

4.) The IRS allows residential investment properties to be depreciated over 27.5 years.

5.) The IRS allows commercial properties to be depreciated over 39 years.

6.) Refinancing is in some respects the most powerful tool that an investor has. It is quick, cost efficient, and tax free.

PART FOUR

THE TIME

YOUR MOST PRECIOUS RESOURCE

CHAPTER 13
DRAFT A DREAM TEAM

"Individual commitment to a group effort — that is what makes a team work, a company work, a society work, a civilization work."

Vince Lombardi

WEALTH ACCUMULATION IS A TEAM SPORT

"Teamwork is the ability to work together toward a common vision; the ability to direct individual accomplishments toward organizational objectives. It is the fuel that allows common people to attain uncommon results."

Andrew Carnegie

If you are going to have any level of measurable success at the highest levels, you are going to need help. This assistance can come in many forms: coaches, consultants, business partners, associates, friends, and, of course, family.

If Michael Jordan, Lance Armstrong, and Tiger Woods, the three most dominant athletes in the past two decades, have used coaches, then you too can benefit from a coach, or at the *least,* business partners.

Remember the old shampoo commercial about dandruff, where one actor asks the next why he uses the dandruff control shampoo. "But you don't have dandruff?" And the reply was something like he didn't have dandruff *because* he used the dandruff control shampoo. Well coaching and business relationships have this same positive effect on helping you achieve success, they make it look easy. They help you to put top spin on your actions.

Just as basketball, cycling, and golf can be played at the highest levels, so too can investing and wealth accumulation; these "sports" are no different. Real estate investing and planning is a team sport. The sooner you learn this, the more money you will make, the quicker you will make it, and the better off you will be.

BUILD YOUR FRANCHISE

By forming a team, you are able to formulate a mastermind group that is of your choosing and at your exclusive benefit that you can work in concert with for the years moving forward. It is your team; think of it as a professional sports franchise. You can have any player or business person you want, as long as you are willing to pay him or her. Clearly, you need to balance your payroll and at the same time maximize your investments in your team, but the reality of it is that in most instances you pay for what you get. Very rarely will a team be able to compete and win unless it has the best players or team members.

Look at the most dominant sport teams over the past decade or so. Most people would say the Yankees and the Lakers are the most recognizable and successful franchises. Not surprisingly, they also consistently go out and sign the best and most expensive players. And before long, the best players want to play for the best teams because the best players want to win. You will find that the more winning you do and the more success you have, the more that successful people want to be around you to help you.

So it is up to you the General Manager, to interview, consult, and draft the members that will make up your franchise. You hire and fire; you reward and discipline your team. You are the President and CEO of your franchise, your mastermind group, your administration. You make it happen.

THE PLAYERS

> *"It is literally true that you can succeed best and quickest by helping others to succeed."*
>
> *Napoleon Hill*

At a bare minimum, your team must be comprised of a Real Estate Planner®, a CPA, a mortgage banker, an insurance agent, and a financial planner. Other business owners that you may want to include would be a contractor for property repairs and an attorney.

At the core of any successful real estate plan or any investing strategy will be a knowledgeable Real Estate Planner®. This is an individual that has knowledge and experience of real estate finance and forecasting well above and beyond that of any other real estate agent or Realtor®. These are individuals that understand the craft of Real Estate Planning® as a financial science not just a simple transaction. This idea, or occupation, is indeed the focus and reason for this book.

One reservation that many individuals have about real estate agents is that the agent will find and keep for him or herself all of the good deals or properties. While admittedly there may be a shred of truth to this concern, the pros far outweigh the cons when it comes to working with a Real Estate Planner®. And as you have hopefully learned by reading this book, this framework is not about finding deals or stealing properties, rather it is about holding properties. The sooner you learn this simple fact, the better results you will have with Real Estate

Planning®. The simple truth is that you make your money with the terms of the acquisition rather than just the price of the acquisition. In essence, it is the holding of the property that makes you money, not the ability to buy at a discount or in the wholesale market.

Real Estate Planners® should also be able to provide another resource for you, property management. As we had discussed in Chapter 7, at some point in time the responsibility of property management should be delegated to a professional. This professional should be your Real Estate Planner®. If they can't do it, then they will know of a company that can.

A CPA will be a critical part of the investing framework. A CPA will assist you in paying fewer taxes by making sure that you are taking advantage of every tax write-off opportunity that is available to you. A CPA is the difference between tax evasion and avoidance. Don't be afraid to invest a significant amount of your payroll into securing the services of a great CPA. They will be worth their weight in gold. I guarantee it.

A good mortgage banker is going to be a very valuable asset. The reality of it is that unless you have a strong relationship with a mortgage banker, it is going to make your life very difficult. This person is your key to getting money. Without him or her, you cannot get your business or investments off the ground.

The beginning stages for this relationship will be the most laborious. However, once you have a relationship and have provided this person with all the necessary information, acquiring properties gets to be a lot more fun.

The significance of a mortgage banker as opposed to a broker is that a banker has complete control over the underwriting and funding process. There should be no surprises. A broker on the other hand, must broker their deals out of house. They are a middle man, a third wheel, a third party; they will not be somebody that you can rely on for the long haul to develop a close relationship with. This person will not be able to make exceptions when they need to be made or pull strings when they need to be pulled.

An insurance agent is somebody that, hopefully, you won't have to talk with too often. The significance is that should something happen on one of your properties, you will want to have somebody you can depend on and communicate with to get the problem resolved. Insurance rates may not always be the best determining factor when choosing an agent.

A Financial Planner is a perfect supplement to a Real Estate Planner®. A strong argument can be made that an investor needs to diversify his or her portfolio with equities and mutual funds and even CD's or bonds. You should hire a Financial Planner to provide you with things like life insurance, a cash reserve account, and perhaps even some disability or long-term care insurance. It also may not be a bad idea to take advantage of various retirement planning funds.

To make your life simple, start developing a relationship with a licensed contractor. The reality is that things in your properties are going to break and need to be fixed or replaced. The contractor will be a person that you can depend on to fix things in a reasonable amount of time at a fair price. Think of it in these terms, you are a business owner; your customer is your tenant. It is your responsibility to make certain that your customer's needs are taken care of and that their living conditions are above average. If you don't do your job and take care of your tenant one of two things will happen; one, your tenant will move out on you, or two, they won't renew their lease with you. Either way you lose money by not servicing your tenants. They pay your mortgage and provide you with a very powerful investment vehicle. The least you can do is to make sure their needs are met in a timely fashion.

An attorney, like an insurance agent, is somebody that hopefully you won't have to talk with too often. The reality of it is that at some point in time you will probably need an attorney. It would behoove you to interview and cultivate a relationship with one now. Consider it like a savings account for a rainy day.

LEVERAGE YOUR WORK AND EXPERTISE

> *"Alone we can do so little; together we can do so much."*
>
> *Helen Keller*

So there it is; these are the positions that need to be filled. It is up to you to interview and eventually draft your team so that you can build your business, investments, and wealth for the years moving forward in an efficient and productive fashion.

Remember, with real estate investing you are not just buying and selling shares of stocks, you are running a business, and with any business you need to have employees, independent contractors, or consultants. You can't do it alone. Leverage the work hours and expertise of your chosen experts; add top spin to your efforts so that you can generate more efficient results for accumulating wealth.

Develop an exclusive relationship with a Real Estate Planner® so they can do the leg work for you and at the same time commit to you 100 percent knowing that you have in return committed yourself to work with them. Hire an accountant so that you can save more money on your taxes and at the same time not have to invest your time to research every tax code on your own. Work with a specific lender so that the qualifying process is simple for every acquisition and you know you are not being taken advantage of. The bottom line is that by establishing a relationship based on trust and open communication, you will be able to expedite the results that you are seeking, and you may even be able to bring to your team the same successes you have experienced! Leverage the knowledge, expertise, and connections of professionals so you can save yourself time and money.

> *"Individuals play the game, but teams beat the odds."*
>
> *SEAL Team saying*

POINTS TO REMEMBER: DRAFT A DREAM TEAM

1.) If you are going to have any level of measurable success at the highest levels you are going to need help. This assistance can come in many forms, coaches, consultants, business partners, associates, friends, and of course family.

2.) By forming a team you are able to formulate a mastermind group that is of your choosing and at your exclusive benefit.

3.) At a bare minimum your team must be comprised of a Real Estate Planner®, a CPA, a mortgage banker, an insurance agent, and a Financial Planner. Other business owners that you may want to include would be a contractor for property repairs and an attorney.

4.) Remember, with real estate investing you are not just buying and selling shares of stocks, you are running a business, and with any business you need to have employees, independent contractors, or consultants.

5.) The driving force behind this investment framework is leverage. Take that principle and apply it to the business and the relationships on your team. Leverage the knowledge, expertise, and connections of professionals so you can save yourself time and money.

CHAPTER 14
MAKING THE CASE

"Do the thing and you will have the power."

Ralph Waldo Emerson

So why should you follow this real estate investment framework? Let's take a shot at the alternative.

The prototypical American has a very predictable financial life. You attend an institution of higher education and obtain an expensive 4-year college degree; it seemed like the right thing to do; it is what everybody else was doing, and it is what your parents wanted you to do. You graduate from college with student loans and credit card debt that you used to pay for food and entertainment while in school because you were too busy studying and making the Dean's list to hold a job at the same time.

You graduate with honors, but the only job you can find upon graduation is bussing tables at a local restaurant. You can't wait tables because you don't have the experience. And you don't have the experience because you were too busy in college getting the grades you thought you needed. The pay for bussing is embarrassing because the restaurant owner knows he can get cheaper labor for three bucks an hour around the corner if you don't want to do it for him.

After bouncing from job to job and barely paying your bills for the first two to four years after graduation, you finally land a job, with no relation to your college degree of course. It pays you well enough to go buy a home and a more reliable car, so you can get yourself deeper in debt. The company provides stock incentive programs so you are feeling pretty good about yourself and the future of your retirement. The problem with the great job is that you also find you are paying an arm and a leg in taxes to Uncle Sam. So you aren't really able to pay off your debt as much as you had hoped, and saving any significant money for retirement other than your minimal contribution to your company 401K is almost comical to you considering your current financial circumstances.

Three or four years go by, and now you decide you want to have a family. And as it turns out, having a family and keeping up with the Jones's can be a real pain in the financial butt. So you buy a larger home in a nicer neighborhood as well as a more luxurious "family" car that starts with a B and ends with a W. Now instead of paying off your debt, or saving for retirement, you are paying for your 2.5 kids, your mortgage, and your car. And of course you want your kids to have *everything* that you never had growing up. So you buy all of these great things for your kids, on credit cards of course, and you continue to red line your monthly cash flow.

Finally, one day, on the eve of sending your kids off to a cheap community college, with the help of financial aid, your boss of 20 years walks into your office and tells you that the company that you work for is going out of business after 50 years. It is due to cheaper overseas labor infringing on the companies margins. They are going to have to let you go. Oh, and by the way, the value of the stock incentives that you had, have vanished into thin air. So now you don't have a job, savings, or a retirement plan, and you are forced to declare bankruptcy. And the only way you are going to be able to send your kids to school is if you drive them there. So your kids have to take out a student loan, just like you did. You are hoping that between social security, which your kids are already paying through *their* noses for, and direct financial support from your kids and *their* college degrees, you will still be able to retire at age 65. And maybe worse case scenario, you will need to find a part-time job as a greeter at a local wholesale company so you can make ends meet.

So why should you follow this traditional plan, why not make it easy on yourself? Upon graduating from high school, get a library card and check out a couple of books on a subject that interest you. Invest what money you do have into the stock of a crippled and bankrupt company, then declare bankruptcy yourself, and go find a job as a greeter. It is just more streamlined this way.

So after reading this far, you are still uncertain? Then here is the case for this real estate framework.

- We know inflation is not going anywhere, but up, to the tune of a little over three percent a year.

- We know that property values nationally have risen over eight percent a year for the last 20 something years.

- We know there is a strong correlation between housing prices and inflation. So if inflation is always on the rise, then so too will the housing market.

- We know the population in the United States continues to rise. This is due to immigration, both legal and illegal, natural population growth, and the fact that people are living longer.

- We know that land is a scarce commodity. "They aren't making any more of it."

- We know that our largest annual bill is our tax bill.

- We know real estate is the only investment that will significantly limit the amount of tax we pay.

- We know we can generate annual returns of between 20-30 percent on real estate investments.
- We know that the equities market may not be as safe as we thought.
- We know at some point in our lives we want to retire. The sooner the better.

POWER

The consensus of these material facts is that there are trends that lean in favor of holding real estate properties for extended periods of time. The trends show real estate is literally the most powerful investment medium. It can perform the greatest amount of work or leveraged appreciation, in the shortest amount of time.

Power = Work/Time

The work that is performed is not based just on the national appreciation of over eight percent, but it also takes into consideration the leverage factor, this equates to 20 to 30 percent annual returns in most instances.

The time is a combination of two factors, your personal investment of time or hours of work, and the time it takes for the investment to reach the desired outcome. In regards to your personal time commitment, there is not much of one. You have leveraged the management responsibilities to a professional. Your Real Estate Planner® finds the properties for you. Your only time commitment is to go to the mailbox and get your check, which is something you are already doing anyways. The time it takes for the investment to reach the desired outcome will be 10 years for most states, fewer years for quite a few states, and more years for very few states.

The reality is that this investment framework or campaign will be successful for all Americans. The average national appreciation is eight percent, the median is 6.7 percent. For some states, the 10-year framework will take fewer years and for others it may just take a little longer. The statistics from the OFHEO show that of the 50 states, all but seven of them have had an annual appreciation greater than four percent a year. Those seven states that did not have an annual appreciation of at least four percent a year are Wyoming, Alaska, Louisiana, North Dakota, West Virginia, Texas, and Oklahoma. For those of you who have been cursed to live in these states of real estate purgatory, there is hope, just keep reading.

Four percent appreciation a year for ten years on a house valued at $150,000 would generate over $70,000 tax free equity over a ten-year period. This is the equivalent of earning a $100,000 a year taxable salary. But now, with real estate, with this framework, you are doing it with the smallest of time commitments. You are able to leverage your time in such a fashion that you are able to create a perpetual wealth building business.

What this means is that there are no excuses for most people as to why they can't follow this framework through to completion. If financial independence and abundance are important to you, and you do live in real estate purgatory, then perhaps you want to think about moving your money or your family or both to a more real estate friendly state. Remember, in 10 years, if you choose to take action, you will have in place a self-perpetuating wealth creating system. Would it make sense to relocate to make this happen? Yes. Would it make sense to invest your money in a different state to make this happen? Yes.

The power of this type of real estate framework cannot be rivaled by traditional investment mediums. As you look at the chart of investment options on the next page, you will notice that even placing your money in a property in Oklahoma, the least profitable real estate state in the country over the last 20 years, will produce a better return on investment than small company growth stocks. These figures, of course, do not include the tax advantages, the principal reduction, or the cash flow that will be generated by the real estate investment; they are based solely and exclusively on appreciation.

REAL ESTATE V. EQUITIES/BONDS
INFORMATION AGE V. INDUSTRIAL AGE

Investment Medium	Initial Investment	Asset Size	Annual Compound Rate of Return	Projected Value in 10 Years
Real Estate @(OK)	#15,000	150,000	*2.87%	^199,057
Real Estate (National)	#15,000	150,000	*8.04%	^325,040
Real Estate !(MA)	#15,000	150,000	*19.66%	^902,778
Small Company Stocks	*15,000*	*15,000*	*12.15%*	*47,215*
Large Company Stocks	*15,000*	*15,000*	*10.20%*	*39,619*
Long-Term Corporate Bonds	*15,000*	*15,000*	*5.90%*	*26,610*
Intermediate-Term Gov't Bonds	*15,000*	*15,000*	*5.44%*	*25,476*
Long-Term Gov't Bonds	*15,000*	*15,000*	*5.45%*	*25,500*
Treasury Bills	*15,000*	*15,000*	*3.79%*	*21,759*
Inflation	*15,000*	*15,000*	*3.05%*	*20,257*

*These rates were sourced and generated from the OFHEO statistics of home values since 1980. (Exhibit 2)

Italic – These rates were sourced from Ibbotson Associates. (Exhibit 11)

The initial real estate investment is based on a 10 percent down payment. This downpayment will allow you in most instances to acquire a property valued at $150,000.

^This figure exclusively represents appreciation only. It does not represent debt reduction or equity build up, tax write-offs, or cash flow that the property generated.

@Oklahoma is the state that has produced the smallest amount of appreciation in the housing market since 1980.

! Massachusetts is the state that has produced the largest amount of appreciation in the housing market since 1980.

The reality is that the stock market was great for the industrial age. Now that we are in the information age, all bets are off, expectations have shifted, the landscape is changing drastically. Information is being disseminated at light speed and unless you are willing to change, adjust, or adapt, *you will* be left behind wondering what happened? The writing is on the wall. This framework is not a knee-jerk reaction or a get rich quick scam. It is a time proven strategy. The numbers do not lie. And you already know this; because the chances are very good that you own your own home. And it has passed the litmus test if you have owned it for any amount of time. You have seen the benefits, the tax write-offs; the powerful appreciation. Why not own another property, and another? Real estate as an investment should be nothing new to you; this framework should not come as a surprise or be a revelation. It is what is prudent and what needs to be done if you expect to get ahead in today's economy.

Today's middle class is being dissolved before our eyes. Our society is turning into the "have" and "have nots."

There is no more standing still; you are either moving up into the upper class, or you are falling into the lower class. Those that have the knowledge and take action on it are leaving their "peers" behind. Information has become the ultimate catalyst for wealth creation, and real estate is the underlying theme of this information.

> *"Man cannot discover new oceans until he has courage to lose sight of the shore."*
>
> *Anonymous*

POINTS TO REMEMBER: MAKING THE CASE

1.) Property values nationally have risen over eight percent a year for the last 20 something years.

2.) There is a strong correlation between housing prices and inflation. So if inflation is always on the rise, then so too will the housing market.

3.) Land is a scarce commodity. "They aren't making any more of it."

4.) Our tax bill is our largest annual bill. Real estate is the only investment medium that will decrease the amount that we pay in tax.

5.) We can generate annual returns of between 20-30 percent on real estate investments.

6.) Real estate is literally the most powerful investment medium. It can perform the greatest amount of work or leveraged appreciation, in the shortest amount of time.

CHAPTER 15
MAKE IT HAPPEN

"The greatest mistake a man can ever make is not making one."

Anonymous

PERPETUAL MOTION

"We are that which we repeatedly do. Excellence, there fore, is not an act but a habit."

Aristotle

In Stephen R. Covey's *The 7 Habits of Highly Effective People,* he talks about how the most successful people all throughout history have had one strikingly similar characteristic, the uncanny ability to be in perpetual motion.

The reason this characteristic is important is two-fold. First, you are able to generate momentum through taking even the smallest of actions. And second, the more you take action, the more successes you will have.

'WE HAVE LIFT OFF!'

"All glory comes from daring to begin."

Anonymous

By daring to begin, you make a commitment to take the first step, to take the smallest of actions to move yourself forward. Once in motion, it becomes *natural* for you to *remain* in motion. Newton's First Law of Motion states than an object in motion will remain in motion unless acted upon by an external force. Once you are in this state of motion or empowerment, it becomes easier for you to continue to take action. These continued actions will surely lead to some disappointments or learning experiences, but the successes you achieve will far outweigh the undesirable outcomes.

Think about the energy the Space Shuttle requires to lift-off and break free from earth's unforgiving gravitational pull. Over seven million pounds of thrust and 85 percent of the shuttle's fuel is used within the first two-minutes of the miraculous lift-off! All of this just to break free and to *start* the voyage to the stars. And then once the shuttle is in motion it can release the additional rockets and soar effortlessly to its orbit 200 miles above the earth's surface.

Often times the most daunting or *impossible* goals are achieved only because *somebody* was emboldened or empowered to take the first step. It is like the saying, "How do you eat an elephant." Of course the answer is, "One bite at a time." Nothing happens unless first an action is taken or an object is put into motion.

BOTTOM LINE

"Far better is to dare mighty things, to win glorious triumphs, even though checkered by failure, than to take rank with those poor spirits who neither enjoy much nor suffer much because they live in the gray twilight that knows not victory or defeat."

Theodore Roosevelt

Success in life is not dependent upon batting averages or percentages, but rather bottom-line numbers. It does not matter how many tries it took you, only that you accomplished what you set out to do. Have you or have you not succeeded? The world does not care what obstacles you had to overcome to accomplish what you have. The world only cares that you have in fact accomplished the goal.

Think about it, does anybody know or care how many at bats it took Hank Aaron, the all-time home-run hitter, to set the current home run record. No, they only know and remember the number 755, the amount of his career home runs.

Or what about Lance Armstrong, putting his victory over cancer aside, do people know how many Tour de Frances he raced in and never won? Or even how many individual stages he lost on his way to winning the tour? Of course not, they remember his five straight tour victories as of 2003.

Even Thomas Edison *failed* over 2,000 times when trying to find the right materials to make the filament for the light bulb. He looked at these attempts not as *failures* but rather progress as he moved forward and closer to making the first light bulb. He literally ran out of ways to not make it work. The only way he had left after 2,000 attempts was the correct way.

Life is not a game of percentages but rather it is a game of bottom lines. The reality is that the more successes you have the more amazing and rewarding your life becomes. Failures and setbacks are only temporary obstacles on your road to an extraordinary life.

Take a look at an apple tree. There might be over a hundred apples on the tree, and each apple has ten seeds. That's a lot of seeds!

We might ask, "Why would you need so many seeds to grow just a few more apple trees?"

Nature has something to teach us here. It's telling us, "Not all seeds grow. In life, most seeds never grow. So if you really want to make something happen, you had better try more than once."

This might mean you'll need to read 20 books on finance and investing before you find one with an initiative that will work for you. That you'll talk to 25 homeowners to find one that will pay for your closing costs or down-payment if you need them to; that you'll interview five people to find one good tenant to lease your property to. Or that it may take you 10 years to become financially independent.

When we understand the "Law of the Seed", we don't get so disappointed. We stop feeling like victims. We learn how to deal with things that happen to us.

Laws of nature are not things to take personally. We just need to understand them and work with them. Successful people fail more often. But they plant more seeds.

RISK TOLERANCE

> *"Act as if it were impossible to fail."*
>
> *Dorothea Brande*

Some of the concepts or strategies in this investment campaign may seem a little risky, dangerous, or even financially hazardous. This tentativeness is a perfectly normal interpretation to some new and powerful concepts. This being said, it is critical to your success that you begin to adjust your thought process and grow your risk tolerance. The most effective way for you to acclimate to these ideas is to start small and try one at a time.

Growing your risk tolerance is very similar to weight training. If I were to tell you to go try to bench press 300 lbs., and you had never even lifted weights before, you would be in denial that you could ever do it. You would not even be able to get the bar off the rack and if you did, you would probably break your rib cage as the weight would come crashing down on you!

Instead, the smart thing for you to do rather than throwing yourself into a dangerous situation and trying to lift 300 lbs. on your first day, would be to start lifting with a lighter weight first, maybe just 100 lbs. And then after a couple weeks or months you could add on more weight, and now maybe you are lifting 150 lbs. You are half-way there already!

Finally, after a couple of years of dedicated training, proper nutrition, and a strong belief system, you are lifting your goal of the 300 lbs. Now that you are at this level and you have increased your strength tolerance, the 100 lbs. you started with seems like nothing, you can barely feel it. Never again will there be a need for you to lift that little amount of weight again. It does nothing to increase your strength and it does not motivate you or challenge you to have a great workout. Your risk tolerance, like a rubber band, has been stretched and it can never return to its original and limiting form.

On a side note, surprisingly to many people, except those that have been there before, you will see the most amazing results in the very beginning of a weight-training regimen. In addition, it is actually a good thing to experience soreness after a workout. This is an indication that you have put your muscles through an intense regimen; you have "broken them down" so that they can then repair themselves and become stronger because of it. This phenomenon is called the overload principal. Your muscles or strength will only grow if you overload the system with more weight or resistance than it has experienced previously. This is also true of increasing your risk tolerance. This first step is clearly the hardest step to take, but you must consistently overload your risk threshold if you want it to continue to grow.

This metaphor applies very clearly to investing in real estate and the concepts that you have learned about in this book. The first property you buy is similar to your first trip to the gym; it is uncomfortable, you feel like everybody is looking at you, and you are worried that everybody is going to laugh at you if you do something the wrong way. The good news is that by taking action and buying your first property, you are well on your way to financial abundance.

Once you have the first property, the other acquisitions will become much easier as you move forward. Each step in the process works as a building block. Just as you can't lift 300 lbs. before you can lift 100 lbs; you can't psychologically buy an apartment complex before you can psychology buy a single family house.

PARALYSIS BY ANALYSIS

> *"Nothing will ever be attempted if all possible objections must be first overcome."*
>
> *Samuel Johnson*

Paralysis by analysis is a very common yet debilitating phenomenon for people trying something new or trying to perform something flawlessly. Real estate investing certainly falls under this umbrella.

The mindset is that a person has to know or understand every concept or must have everything perfect before taking action or acquiring a property. This analysis can absolutely kill your motivation to take action.

Clearly, before making a commitment to invest in real estate, you are going to have to do your homework. You perform a Comparative Market Analysis, a Rental Comparative Market Analysis, a Monthly Cash Flow

Analysis, an Annual Financial Forecast, and a Monthly Profit and Loss Statement. Once these are completed, and it makes sense, you take action, without delay.

The problem that some people run into is that they begin to acquire "the sky is falling" mentality. They imagine that anything that could go wrong, will go wrong. They want it to be more perfect, more fool-proof. They begin to think about not having enough reserves allocated for the property. They worry about paying too much in property taxes for new schools. They begin to think about whether or not it is a good rental market or a good time of the year to rent a property. They think it will never rent, and that if it does rent, that the tenants will destroy the property. Or they worry that the $25 a month they are in the red each month is going to bankrupt them.

Here is the reality; things are never going to be perfect. You can never hedge against every calamity. That is the nature of this type of investment or any other investment for that matter. That is why they call them investments and not gifts.

To move forward through these objections you establish a three to six-month mortgage reserve for each property. You understand that a 20-30 percent return on investment will over-shadow the couple hundred extra dollars you may have to pay in taxes for new schools to be built. You understand that there will never be a perfect market for property owners. If interest rates are low, the rental market is soft but your debt service is smaller. If interest rates are higher more people will be renting but your debt service will increase significantly, and you may not be able to acquire a property at all. And, of course, you can never predict what time of year somebody will need to find a place to rent. People sell homes, and relocate at all times throughout the year. Hazard Insurance, the security deposit and cleaning deposits will help cover the unlikely damages that may have been done to your property. And finally, the $25 a month you are in the red will be recouped at the end of the year through your tax-write-offs. Think of it as your investment into paying off the debt service to the property.

If you want a 100 percent secure investment, go back down to the minor leagues and put your money in a CD or Bond or savings account. If you want to retire in 10 years you have to play in the major leagues and invest your money in this framework.

"There Is No Tomorrow!"

"Every great and commanding moment in the annals of the world is the triumph of some enthusiasm."

Ralph Waldo Emerson

Apollo Creed, played by Carl Weathers, said this to Rocky, Sylvester Stallone, during the Rocky III movie. It was at a time when Rocky was training for his upcoming bout with Clubber Lang, played by Mr. T. Rocky had lost "the eye of the tiger," and Creed needed to give Rocky a wake-up call to do it now! Either Rocky would do it now, today, or he should forget about defeating Lang. There is no tomorrow!

Eliminate the word "tomorrow" from your vocabulary. If you substituted every "tomorrow" for a "today" or even a "Tuesday" or a *specific* day, you would take action much more frequently and you would increase your results ten-fold. Although there is a limit to how much we can fit into a 24-hour day, my guess is that very few people are even close to 100 percent productivity. By eliminating "tomorrow," procrastination will cease to exist and your productivity will explode.

The bottom line is that you must make every decision set in stone, make a commitment, make it a *must*. It is not enough to *want* to do something, or to say to yourself that you *should* do something. You must develop an absolute conviction that you *must* do it. There are an abundance of people in the world who would like to have more money, improved health, a different life, a life of their dreams, but they never make the conviction to make the change. Be one of the few that commits to take action to make a change in your life.

STAY THE COURSE

> *"He that can't endure the bad; will not live to see the good."*
>
> *Jewish Proverb*

Abraham Lincoln the 16th President of the United States, and perhaps one of the more accomplished Presidents, had to endure an incredible amount of obstacles on his road to the Presidency.

At age 21, he failed in business
At age 22, he was defeated in a legislative race
At age 24, he failed in business
At age 26, his sweetheart died
At age 27, he had a nervous breakdown
At age 34, he was defeated in a Congressional race
At age 36, he was defeated in a Congressional race
At age 45, he lost a Senatorial race
At age 47, he failed in an effort to win the VP
At age 49, he lost a Senatorial race
At age 52, he won the Presidency of the U.S.

His road was clearly a test of endurance and perseverance. Think about how easy it would have been for him to have quit at age 27 when he had a nervous breakdown or at 36 when he lost his second congressional race. Lincoln understood that it was not the number of failures he experienced, but rather the number of times he took a hit, got the wind knocked out of him, and got back in the ring. He stayed the course.

"Success is the ability to go from one failure to another with no loss of enthusiasm."

Sir Winston Churchill

For many successful people it is a matter of not necessarily avoiding obstacles, but rather what you decide to do with those obstacles and setbacks that are the defining moments in a person's life. It is the price they paid along the way that got them to where they are today. It is their ability or refusal to give up or quit when other people would have already thrown in the towel, packed their bags, put their tail between their legs, and walked home. It is really the *setbacks* that have *allowed* them to get where they are and experience the successes that they have had. As the saying goes, if it were easy, then everybody would be doing it.

On The Right Track

Often times a word, a speech, or an oration can let someone know they are on the right track; it can literally drive someone to action or change a life. The following words will hopefully be able to inspire and perhaps more importantly empower *you* to take action.

"Many of life's failures are people who did not realize how close they were to success when they gave up."

Thomas A. Edison

"We will either find a way or make one."

Hannibal

"This thing that we call "failure" is not the falling down, but the staying down."

Mary Pickford

"All things are difficult before they're easy."

Thomas Fuller

"Obstacles cannot crush me. Every obstacle yields to stern resolve. He who is fixed to a star does not change his mind."

Leonardo da Vinci

"Go confidently in the direction of your dreams. Live the life you have imagined."

Henry David Thoreau

Points to Remember: Make it Happen

1.) In Stephen R. Covey's *The 7 Habits of Highly Effective People,* he talks about how the most successful people all throughout history have had one strikingly similar characteristic, the uncanny ability to be in perpetual motion.

2.) By daring to begin, you make a commitment to take the first step, to take the smallest of actions to move yourself forward. Once in motion, it becomes *natural* for you to *remain* in motion.

3.) Success in life is not dependent upon batting averages or percentages, but rather bottom-line numbers. It does not matter how many tries it took you, only that you accomplished what you set out to do.

4.) It is critical to your success that you begin to adjust your thought process and grow your risk tolerance.

5.) Paralysis by analysis is a very common and debilitating phenomenon for people trying something new or trying to perform something flawlessly. Real estate investing certainly falls under this umbrella.

6.) Take the word "tomorrow" out of your vocabulary. If you substituted every "tomorrow" for a "today" or even a "Tuesday" or specific day, you would take action much more frequently and you would increase your results ten fold.

CHAPTER 16
PAY IT FORWARD

"The great aim of education is not knowledge but action."

Herbert Spencer

The title of this chapter was taken from the movie *Pay it Forward*, directed by Mimi Leder and produced by Steven Reuther. The movie is a wonderful story about the power that we have within us to change our world. And most importantly to contribute and expect nothing in return. The following story gives us a perspective of this.

There was once a wealthy landowner who lived in a stately mansion overlooking a huge piece of property with a beautiful valley. Although the landowner had this material wealth, he also had emptiness in his life. He had no religious beliefs, he lived alone, and he was possessed by his material gains.

His farm manager John, and his family, lived in a small cottage on his estate. John was a man of simple faith and deep religious commitment. He attended church regularly with his family and the Lord's presence was a reality in his home. John was frequently seen helping the less fortunate, welcoming the stranger, and visiting and caring for the sick. If the landowner happened to go by the manager's cottage in the evening, he often noticed John's family on their knees in prayer.

One sunny and glorious morning the landowner rose early and was gazing out onto his beautiful valley through his bedroom window. He said to himself, "This is all mine." Suddenly he heard the doorbell ring. He went downstairs and answered the door. There was his manager on his doorstep. "What's the matter John," he asked? John looked embarrassed. "Sir, could I have a word with you?" John hesitated and finally said, "I had a terribly vivid dream last night. The Lord appeared to me and told me that the richest man in the valley would die tonight at midnight. I just had to come to you. I thought you should know."

The landowner dismissed John's concern, but afterwards his words kept bothering him; so much so that he immediately went to the local doctor for a complete checkup. The doctor examined him, pronounced him "fit as a fiddle" and said he was good for another twenty years. The landowner was relieved but a lingering doubt caused him to invite the doctor around for dinner and a few drinks that evening so he'd be with him at midnight.

When midnight passed and nothing happened, he saw the doctor to the door, thanked him, and went upstairs muttering to himself, "Silly old John, he upset my whole day, him and his dreams."

No sooner was the landowner in bed than he heard the doorbell ringing. It was just after midnight. Answering the door, he found John's sobbing teenage daughter at the door. "Sir," she said, looking at him through her tears, "My mother sent me to tell you that Daddy died, just at midnight."

Suddenly it was clear to him who was the richest man in the valley. It was John, the man of simple faith and deep commitment to the service of others, who had wisely stored treasure up for himself in Heaven.*

*This story was the homily that was read by Father William Kaliyadn at my Dad's funeral in September of 2001. It is significant because it is the theme of this chapter, Pay it Forward.

"You can't live a perfect day without doing something for someone who will never be able to repay you."

John Wooden

Part Four of this book has been about time, our most precious resource. It has been about leveraging the expertise and the time of professionals; it has been about why this framework is the most powerful investment campaign; and it has explained the wonder of inertia and momentum, and of having a sense of urgency. And so this last chapter, *Pay it Forward,* is about just that, time, not only your time but the time of your family and others in your community.

This chapter is intended to have you begin to think bigger than just you and your needs; to begin to think about family and community and how to help those around you. The desire for a need to contribute, to give back, is the ultimate indication of possessing true wealth.

It is impossible to be wealthy if you are not in a psychological state of abundance. No money will ever be sufficient, nor house big enough to compensate for a feeling of scarcity. The only way to overcome a feeling of scarcity is to begin paying it forward now and not wait for the right time. There will never be the right time.

Don't wait for 10 years to contribute. Don't wait until you are financially independent, secure, free from car loans, and credit card debt, free from having to ever work another day in your life. Do it now.

This invitation to contribute can come in a multitude of forms; your time, your money, a gift, guidance, or even a thank you.

Perhaps you can share what you have learned about this framework not only with your kids and perhaps your grand-kids but to other people that are looking for a better life.

THE "QUAN"

Live your life with the "Quan." Some of you may recognize this word from the movie *Jerry Maguire*. The "Quan" is a word that Rod Tidwell, played by Cuba Gooding Jr., uses to represent the whole package in life. Anybody can follow this investment framework and make money and be successful and have a good life, but when all cylinders are going you will have in your possession the "Quan."

The "Quan" is financial independence without the 70 and 80 hour work weeks and stress, it is gaining the respect of others with no intention of doing so, it is giving time and love to your family and those in need of it without expecting a thing in return. It is being healthy and free from disease and addiction. It is giving without being asked to give, donating and expecting nothing in return. It is living a life well-lived. It is living the life that you have imagined. It is the whole package. You will know it once you have achieved this. You will feel abundance in every corner of your world.

A LEGACY

> *"We must use time as a tool, not as a crutch."*
>
> *John F. Kennedy*

How do you want to be remembered? You have the power within you to achieve something truly great, to make positive contributions to your family and community. The possibility lies within you. You have the power to make the people around you and the world better because you were here.

Perhaps one of the most empowering questions you can ask yourself is what kind of a legacy do you want to leave behind? How do you want to impact the generations that will come after you? Do you want to make monetary donations, mentor a child, establish charitable funds and programs, or just give of your time to those in need?

Begin to live the life that you have imagined, immediately. The train is not going to come in. You will not wake up one day and be a changed person. The actions and thoughts that you make today will be with you the rest of your life unless you change them *today*.

There is no better time than today to make the change. The common misconception for many people is that they would like to wait for the right time, when things will be perfect, when the planets will be in alignment; these individuals will be waiting forever. Things will never be perfect or just right; the perfect opportunity may never happen. Begin today as though there were no tomorrow.

The longer you wait to take action, the more reasons you will find as to why you shouldn't do it, and thus the harder it will be for you to finally commit to take action. Do not listen to that voice in your head that says you can't, that you are too old or too young, too poor, or too uneducated. Once you listen to the voice it begins to gain in strength and before you know it you will be literally paralyzed to take action. You should be so busy taking action that you will not have the time to listen to the voice. The key to this campaign is the opportunities that will be presented to you. You will only become aware of these opportunities if you are on the field and playing the game.

You are the possibility, the human spirit lies within you, if you tap into the power of your mind; you can and will achieve anything and everything you desire.

And so, if you have come this far, then perhaps you are willing to come a little further. This is not the end but rather the beginning for you. You have learned what it takes to achieve financial independence, now take the next step and begin your journey. My sincere hope is that this book has been able in some way to inspire you to take action on *something, anything*. At the least you owe it to yourself to do something *different* than you have ever done, something different from what other people are doing, be original. If you are going to do something, do it now. And if not now, when? *Now* is the time, now is *always* the time. Today is the first day of the rest of your life, get excited and make it happen! I look forward to hearing about your success!

"While we stop to think, we often miss our opportunity."

Publilius Syrus

POINTS TO REMEMBER: PAY IT FORWARD

1.) The desire for a need to contribute, to give back, is the ultimate indication of possessing true wealth.

2.) Perhaps one of the most empowering questions you can ask yourself is what kind of a legacy do you want to leave behind? How do you want to impact the generations that will come after you? Do you want to make monetary donations, mentor a child, establish charitable funds and programs, or just give of your time to those in need?

3.) You are the possibility, the human spirit lies within you, if you tap into the power of your mind; you can and will achieve anything and everything you desire.

4.) And so if you are going to do something, do it now!

APPENDIX

EXHIBIT 1:

GLOSSARY

Adjustable Rate Mortgage – An ARM is a broad term for any mortgage in which the interest rates and generally the payments change over the life of the loan. The interest rate adjusts to match the fall or rise of a predetermined interest rate index. The borrower's regular payments will decrease or increase accordingly.

Adjusted Basis – This is equal to the acquisition cost plus any capital improvements, minus any depreciation taken.

Amortization – The systematic and continuous repayment of an obligation through periodic installments until the debt has been paid off in full.

Appreciation – An increase in the value of the property. Usually the result of an increase in demand or in some instances the improvements made to the property or neighborhood.

Assumption – A means by which the title or mortgage may be transferred to another party with or without release of liability of a note.

Balloon Payment – This is a lump sum or payment that is larger than the regular monthly payments. It is usually used in a note to reduce some or all, of the principal portion for a required early payoff.

Blue Chip Properties – A new property in a clean and safe subdivision with freeway proximity.

CAP Rate – A rate of return that is used to determine the capital value of an income stream. The formula is: the property value is equal to the net annual income divided by the capitalization rate.

Closing Costs – These are costs in addition to the price of the property that are due at the time of closing. They will include origination fees, discount fees, attorney fees, title insurance, surveys, the recording of documents, and pre-payments of real estate taxes and hazard insurance premiums held by the lender in an impound account.

Comparative Market Analysis – A CMA shows what similar types of properties have sold in a specific area or subdivision over a specific time frame (usually six months), as well as what properties are currently under contract and still on the market (Competitive). The leading indicator is the list price or amount of dollars per square foot.

Competitive Market Analysis – See Comparative Market Analysis.

Conventional Loan – A mortgage loan not insured by the Federal Housing Administration or guaranteed by the Veteran's Administration. It is termed "conventional" because it conforms to accepted standards. No governmental agency approval is necessary of the lender, borrower, or property.

Debt-to-Income Ratio – An income analysis used by the lender to decide how much to lend to the borrower. There are two methods; one compares the amount of *total* monthly expenses to the monthly income and the other compares *only* the amount of the proposed monthly mortgage payment to the monthly income.

Department of Housing and Urban Development (HUD) – This is a department within the government that is responsible for the implementation and administration of government housing and urban development programs.

Depreciation – The allocation of the cost of an asset over its estimated productive life. For residential properties it is 27.5 years, for commercial properties it is 39 years.

Down Payment – This is the difference between the amount of the mortgage and the sales price of the property.

Due-on-Sale Clause – This is a clause within a mortgage agreement that requires the buyer to pay off the mortgage if the property is transferred or sold.

Equity – The amount of cash the owner has realized, paid in, or invested in the property.

Federal Housing Administration – The FHA is a federal agency within the U.S. Department of Housing and Urban Development (HUD). They use loan insurance programs to insure mortgages for lenders. The FHA promotes the availability of housing for low and moderate income families.

FHA Mortgage – A mortgage with mortgage guarantee insurance that is federally sponsored through the FHA.

Fixed Interest Rate – A feature of the mortgage that structures the loan so that there will not be any increases or decreases in the interest rate over the term of the loan.

Flip a Property – The process of acquiring a property, usually at a discount, and immediately transferring the ownership to another party, usually for profit.

Hazard Insurance – This is a form of casualty insurance coverage for real estate. It includes protection against loss, vandalism, fire, and certain natural causes.

Income Property - A rental property with a very strong equity position, it allows for massive cash flow. This type of property has a weak return on equity and minimal tax write-off opportunities. See also Racehorse.

Interest-Only Loans – These are mortgage loans in which only the interest portion of the principal and interest payment is made for a pre-determined period of time. This time period may be as little as two or three years or up to ten years.

Interest Rate – This is the charge for borrowing money. It is commonly expressed as a percentage or an annual rate.

Investment Property – A rental property with a very weak equity position, it allows for very little if any cash flow. This type of property has a strong return on equity and massive tax write-off opportunities. An investment property is used to build the greatest amount of wealth in the shortest amount of time. See also workhorse.

IRC 121 – Internal Revenue Code 121 that pertains to the tax free capital gain for property owners. This code is a product of the Taxpayer Relief Act of 1997. It allows for a tax free capital gain or exclusion of up to $500,000 for joint filers and $250,000 for single filers that have lived in and owned their primary residence for two of the past five years. This exclusion is available once every two years.

IRC 1031 – Internal Revenue Code section 1031 that pertains to like-kind exchanges. It indicates that taxes will not be triggered as they would ordinarily be in the event of a traditional sale. A 1031 exchange provides a safe harbor from paying capital gains taxes and depreciation recapture as long as certain guidelines are followed. Namely, the property or properties you are acquiring need to be of equal to or greater value than the relinquished property, they need to be named within 45 days of the sale of the relinquished property, and closed on within 180 days.

Loan to Value – This is a measure of the amount of total financing relative to the value or sales price of the property.

PITI – Principal, Interest, Taxes, and Insurance. These are the components of the total mortgage payment.

Prepayment Penalty – A monetary penalty under a mortgage, deed of trust, or note, when the loan is paid off before the loan's maturity date.

Qualified Intermediary – A company or person hired to facilitate a 1031 exchange. The party does this by creating the supporting documentation and holding the proceeds from the sale of the relinquished property, on behalf of the individual (tax payer) performing the exchange, until the purchase of the new property is complete.

Racehorse – A rental property with a very strong equity position that allows for massive cash flow. This type of property has a weak return on equity and minimal tax write-off opportunities. See also income property.

RCMA – A Rental Comparative or Competitive Market Analysis; shows what similar types of rental properties have rented for in a specific area or subdivision over a specific time frame (usually six months), as well as what rental properties are currently on the market. The leading indicator is the annual income, in dollars, per square foot.

Real Estate Planner® – A licensed Realtor® that is skilled in real estate acquisition, financc, forccasting, investment, and at finding opportunities for individuals to decrease the amount of tax they pay.

Return on Equity – ROE is a ratio that describes the amount of money that is created per dollars of equity in a property. The return on equity equation is always changing because the equity in the property is always increasing via appreciation and debt reduction. All else being equal, the ROE will decrease every year for as long as the owner has the property.

Return on Investment - A ratio that describes the amount of money that is created per the total amount of dollars originally invested.

Term – The time period for repayment of the loan.

Trickle up Investing – A term used to describe a long term holding strategy for real estate. Although real estate appreciation nationally has been less than the equities market; it also takes less money to acquire a larger asset. So while it may look like insignificant returns, the end result is massive capital growth.

Workhorse - A rental property with a very weak equity position, it allows for very little if any cash flow. This type of property has a strong return on equity and massive tax write-off opportunities. A workhorse is used to build the greatest amount of wealth in the shortest amount of time. See also investment property.

EXHIBIT 2:

PERCENT CHANGE IN HOUSE PRICES

OFFICE OF FEDERAL HOUSING ENTERPRISE OVERSIGHT

PERIOD ENDED DECEMBER 31, 2002

State	*1-Yr.	1-Yr.	Qtr.	5-Yr.	Since 1980
Rhode Island, (RI)	1	15.72	2.5	58.27	296.1
District of Columbia, (DC)	2	12.42	1.12	79.11	244.9
New Jersey, (NJ)	3	11.79	1.18	51.22	267.2
California, (CA)	4	11.46	2.04	67.04	254.7
New Hampshire, (NH)	5	11.02	1.22	68.17	264.5
Maryland, (MD)	6	10.82	1.27	37.95	202.8
Massachusetts, (MA)	7	10.81	1.68	71.89	452.2
New York, (NY)	8	10.6	0.87	53.09	343
Florida, (FL)	9	9.79	1.7	45.16	164.7

Connecticut, (CT)	10	9.43	1.38	46.35	241.2
Maine, (ME)	11	9.08	0.32	48.08	250
Delaware, (DE)	12	8.52	1.14	36	229.5
Virginia, (VA)	13	8.45	0.59	39.31	190.6
Minnesota, (MN)	14	8.07	0.71	54.17	189.1
Hawaii, (HI)	15	7.53	0.07	21.87	184.9
Pennsylvania, (PA)	16	7.39	0.93	28.44	185.1
United States **	**.**	**6.89**	**0.83**	**38.29**	**184.9**
Nevada, (NV)	17	6.53	0.71	24.38	125.4
Montana, (MT)	18	6.4	0.21	23.9	137.5
Vermont, (VT)	19	5.89	-0.13	35.3	203.2
Wyoming, (WY)	20	5.88	-0.39	24.72	78.6
Alaska, (AK)	22	5.64	-0.6	19.91	72.09
Arizona, (AZ)	21	5.64	0.8	32.67	134.5
Illinois, (IL)	23	5.27	0.47	28.71	178.3
Missouri, (MO)	24	5.02	0.53	29.98	141.4

Oregon, (OR)	25	4.69	0.4	22.92	185.2
North Dakota, (ND)	26	4.43	0.09	19.95	84.24
New Mexico, (NM)	27	4.39	0.35	15.63	124.6
Louisiana, (LA)	28	4.37	0.85	25.12	82.78
Colorado, (CO)	29	4.36	0.16	47.93	218.7
Washington, (WA)	30	4.35	0.33	31.27	210.8
South Dakota, (SD)	31	4.26	0.68	24.09	126.3
West Virginia, (WV)	32	4.22	0.35	20.79	91.35
Wisconsin, (WI)	33	4.2	0.36	27.1	153.2
Georgia, (GA)	34	4.15	0.58	35.12	173.6
Kansas, (KS)	35	3.98	0.2	28.51	107.2
Arkansas, (AR)	36	3.77	0.94	20.42	107.2
Michigan, (MI)	37	3.63	0.24	33.49	190.7
Kentucky, (KY)	38	3.49	0.8	24.1	147

Ohio, (OH)	39	3.48	0.59	23.77	145.8
Texas, (TX)	40	3.45	0.31	30.82	84.2
Idaho, (ID)	41	3.33	0.74	18.33	123
South Carolina, (SC)	42	3.25	0.3	28.74	152.3
Oklahoma, (OK)	43	3.21	0.5	24.45	66.14
Alabama, (AL)	44	3.14	0.48	21.74	126.9
Iowa, (IA)	45	3.08	0.43	24.46	110.4
North Carolina, (NC)	46	3	0.27	23.3	169.6
Tennessee, (TN)	47	2.88	0.38	21.58	141.6
Mississippi, (MS)	48	2.83	0.65	22.54	105.4
Indiana, (IN)	49	2.61	0.08	20.11	130.2
Nebraska, (NE)	50	2.6	-0.01	21.31	125.4
Utah, (UT)	51	1.61	0.21	13.53	157.9

Note: Rankings based on annual percentage change.

***** Note: United States figures based on weighted division average.***

EXHIBIT 3:

RETURN ON EQUITY CHART
4% ANNUAL APPRECIATION

Property Value	Equity Chart	Annual ROE
$100,000	1%	400%
$100,000	4%	133%
$100,000	5%	80%
$100,000	10%	40%
$100,000	15%	27%
$100,000	20%	20%
$100,000	25%	16%
$100,000	30%	13%
$100,000	40%	10%
$100,000	50%	8%
$100,000	60%	7%
$100,000	70%	6%
$100,000	80%	5%
$100,000	90%	4%
$100,000	100%	4%

RETURN ON EQUITY CHART
6% ANNUAL APPRECIATION

Property Value	Equity Chart	Annual ROE
$100,000	1%	600%
$100,000	3%	200%
$100,000	5%	120%
$100,000	10%	60%
$100,000	15%	40%
$100,000	20%	30%
$100,000	25%	24%
$100,000	30%	20%

$100,000	40%	15%
$100,000	50%	12%
$100,000	60%	10%
$100,000	70%	9%
$100,000	80%	8%
$100,000	90%	7%
$100,000	100%	6%

RETURN ON EQUITY CHART
8% ANNUAL APPRECIATION

Property Value	Equity Chart	Annual ROE
$100,000	1%	800%
$100,000	3%	267%
$100,000	5%	160%
$100,000	10%	80%
$100,000	15%	53%
$100,000	20%	40%
$100,000	25%	32%
$100,000	30%	27%
$100,000	40%	20%
$100,000	50%	16%
$100,000	60%	13%
$100,000	70%	11%
$100,000	80%	10%
$100,000	90%	9%
$100,000	100%	8%

RETURN ON EQUITY CHART
10% ANNUAL APPRECIATION

Home Value	Equity Chart	Annual ROE
$100,000	1%	1000%
$100,000	3%	333%
$100,000	5%	200%

$100,000	10%	100%
$100,000	15%	67%
$100,000	20%	50%
$100,000	25%	40%
$100,000	30%	33%
$100,000	40%	25%
$100,000	50%	20%
$100,000	60%	17%
$100,000	70%	14%
$100,000	80%	13%
$100,000	90%	11%
$100,000	100%	10%

RETURN ON EQUITY CHART
12% ANNUAL APPRECIATION

Property Value	Equity Chart	Annual ROE
$100,000	1%	1200%
$100,000	3%	400%
$100,000	5%	240%
$100,000	10%	120%
$100,000	15%	80%
$100,000	20%	60%
$100,000	25%	48%
$100,000	30%	40%
$100,000	40%	30%
$100,000	50%	24%
$100,000	60%	20%
$100,000	70%	17%
$100,000	80%	15%
$100,000	90%	13%
$100,000	100%	12%

EXHIBIT 4:

EQUITY GROWTH
4% ANNUAL APPRECIATION

Property Value	Property Value In 5 Years	Property Value In 10 Years
$100,000	$121,665	$148,024
$125,000	$152,081	$185,030
$150,000	$182,497	$222,036
$175,000	$212,914	$259,042
$200,000	$243,330	$296,048

EQUITY GROWTH
6% ANNUAL APPRECIATION

Property Value	Property Value In 5 Years	Property Value In 10 Years
$100,000	$133,822	$179,084
$125,000	$167,278	$223,855
$150,000	$200,733	$268,627
$175,000	$234,189	$313,398
$200,000	$267,645	$358,169

Equity Growth 8% Annual Appreciation

Property Value	Property Value In 5 Years	Property Value In 10 Years
$100,000	$146,932	$215,892
$125,000	$183,666	$269,865
$150,000	$220,399	$323,838
$175,000	$257,132	$377,811
$200,000	$293,865	$431,784

Equity Growth 10% Annual Appreciation

Property Value	Property Value In 5 Years	Property Value In 10 Years
$100,000	$161,051	$259,374
$125,000	$201,313	$324,217
$150,000	$241,576	$389,061
$175,000	$281,839	$453,904

$200,000	$322,102	$518,748

EQUITY GROWTH
12% ANNUAL APPRECIATION

Property Value	Property Value In 5 Years	Property Value In 10 Years
$100,000	$176,234	$310,584
$125,000	$220,292	$388,231
$150,000	$264,351	$465,877
$175,000	$308,409	$543,523
$200,000	$352,468	$621,169

EXHIBIT 5:

THE RULE OF 72
THE NUMBER OF YEARS IT WILL TAKE TO DOUBLE YOUR RETURN AT A GIVEN RATE OF RETURN

Rate of Return	Years to Double
4%	18
6%	12
8%	9
10%	7.2
12%	6
14%	5.1
16%	4.5

EXHIBIT 6:

2002 FEDERAL PERSONAL INCOME TAX RATES

Tax Rate	Single Filers	Married Filing Jointly
10%	up to $6,000	up to $12,000
15%	$6,001 - $27,950	$12,001 - $46,700
25%	$27,951 - $67,700	$46,701 - $112,850
28%	$67,701 - $141,250	$112,851 - $171,950
33%	$141,251 - $307,050	$171,951 - $307,050
35%	$307,051 or more	$307,051 or more

Tax Rate	Married Filing Sep.	Head of Household
10%	up to $6,000	up to $10,000
15%	$6,001 - $23,350	$10,001 - $37,450
25%	$23,351 - $56,425	$37,451 - $96,700
28%	$56,426 - $85,975	$96,701 - $156,600
33%	$85,976 - $153,525	$156,601 - $307,050
35%	$153,526 or more	$307,051 or more

EXHIBIT 7:

HISTORICAL INTEREST RATES

FREDDIE MAC SURVEY OF COMMITMENT RATE AND POINTS, MONTHLY AVERAGE 30-YEAR FIXED-RATE MORTGAGES SINCE 1972

Year	Rate	Points
*2003	5.76	0.6
2002	6.54	0.6
2001	6.97	0.9
2000	8.05	1.0
1999	7.44	1.0
1998	6.94	1.1
1997	7.60	1.7
1996	7.81	1.0
1995	7.93	1.8
1994	8.38	1.8
1993	7.31	1.6
1992	8.39	1.7
1991	9.25	1.0
1990	10.13	2.1
1989	10.32	2.1
1988	10.34	2.1
1987	10.21	2.2
1986	10.19	2.0
1985	12.43	2.5
1984	13.88	2.5
1983	13.24	2.1
1982	16.04	2.2
1981	16.63	2.0
1980	13.74	1.8
1979	11.20	1.6
1978	9.64	1.3
1977	8.85	1.1
1976	8.87	1.0
1975	9.05	1.1

1974	9.19	1.2
1973	8.04	1.0
1972	7.38	0.9
Annual Average	**9.62**	**1.5**

**Through May 2003*

EXHIBIT 8:

ANNUAL SALES OF NEW HOMES 1963-2002

HOUSES SOLD DURING YEAR

Year	Total	Avg. Sales Price	Median Sales Price
2002	974,000	$228,300	$187,100
2001	908,000	$213,200	$175,200
2000	877,000	$207,000	$169,000
1999	880,000	$195,600	$161,000
1998	886,000	$181,900	$152,500
1997	804,000	$176,200	$146,000
1996	757,000	$166,400	$140,000
1995	667,000	$158,700	$133,900
1994	670,000	$154,500	$130,000
1993	666,000	$147,700	$126,500
1992	610,000	$144,100	$121,500
1991	509,000	$147,200	$120,000
1990	534,000	$149,800	$122,900
1989	650,000	$148,800	$120,000
1988	676,000	$138,300	$112,500
1987	671,000	$127,200	$104,500
1986	750,000	$111,900	$92,000
1985	688,000	$100,800	$84,300
1984	639,000	$97,600	$79,900
1983	623,000	$89,800	$75,300
1982	412,000	$83,900	$69,300
1981	436,000	$83,000	$68,900
1980	545,000	$76,400	$64,600
1979	709,000	$71,800	$62,900
1978	817,000	$62,500	$55,700
1977	819,000	$54,200	$48,800
1976	646,000	$48,000	$44,200
1975	549,000	$42,600	$39,300
1974	519,000	$38,900	$35,900
1973	634,000	$35,500	$32,500
1972	718,000	$30,500	$27,600

1971	656,000	$28,300	$25,200
1970	485,000	$26,600	$23,400
1969	448,000	$27,900	$25,600
1968	490,000	$26,600	$24,700
1967	487,000	$24,600	$22,700
1966	461,000	$23,300	$21,400
1965	575,000	$21,500	$20,000
1964	565,000	$20,500	$18,900
1963	560,000	$19,300	$18,000

Source: U.S. Census Bureau

EXHIBIT 9:

HISTORICAL INCOME TABLES
ALL HOUSEHOLDS

Year	No. of Households	Median Income	Mean Income
2001	109,297	42,228	58,208
2000	108,209	41,990	57,135
1999	106,418	42,151	57,047
1998	104,705	40,816	54,842
1997	103,874	38,885	51,855
1996	101,018	35,492	47,123
1995	99,627	34,076	44,938
1994	98,990	32,264	43,133
1993	97,107	31,241	41,428
1992	96,426	30,636	38,840
1991	95,669	30,126	37,922
1990	94,312	29,943	37,403
1989	93,347	28,906	36,520
1988	92,830	27,225	34,017
1987	91,124	26,061	32,410
1986	89,479	24,897	30,759
1985	88,458	23,618	29,066
1984	86,789	22,415	27,464
1983	85,407	20,885	25,401
1982	83,918	20,171	24,309
1981	83,527	19,074	22,787
1980	82,368	17,710	21,063

Source: U.S. Census Bureau

EXHIBIT 10:

ANNUAL RATE OF INFLATION 1970-2003

Year	Annual Percent (Rate of Inflation)
1970	5.7
1971	4.4
1972	3.2
1973	6.2
1974	11.0
1975	9.1
1976	5.8
1977	6.5
1978	7.6
1979	11.3
1980	13.5
1981	10.3
1982	6.2
1983	3.2
1984	4.3
1985	3.6

1986	1.9
1987	3.6
1988	4.1
1989	4.8
1990	5.4
1991	4.2
1992	3.0
1993	3.0
1994	2.6
1995	2.8
1996	2.9
1997	2.3
1998	1.6
1999	2.2
2000	3.4
2001	2.8
2002	1.6
*2003	2.1
Average	**4.9**

Source: U.S. Department of Labor

EXHIBIT 11:

WEALTH INDICES OF INVESTMENTS IN THE U.S. CAPITAL MARKETS 1926-2002

Investment Medium	Annual Compound Rate of Return
Small Company Stocks	12.15%
Large Company Stocks	10.20%
Long-Term Corporate Bonds	5.90%
Intermediate-Term Gov't Bonds	5.44%
Long-Term Government Bonds	5.45%
Treasury Bills	3.79%
Inflation	3.05%

Source: Ibbotson Associates

ORDERING INFORMATION

To order a copy of this and or other books by Mark MacKenzie, go to TheNewGoldRush.biz. This web site will allow you to purchase other *Capitalist Series* books, the Real Estate Planning® Software, find out how to attend The New Gold Rush Seminar®, or contact Mark for an independent Real Estate Planning® consultation.

ABOUT THE AUTHOR

At 26 Mark P. Mac Kenzie is a member of the next generation of real estate superstars. His maverick philosophies on real estate and finance are allowing more and more people to begin to take massive action towards achieving financial independence.

Mark resides in Phoenix, Arizona where he is a licensed Realtor®. He consults and conducts seminars in the field Real Estate Planning® for both seasoned investors and 1st time home buyers alike. Mark continues to work on a transaction basis with select individuals that are committed to improving their net worth.

The New Gold Rush – Real Estate, is the first book in a series of books titled the *Capitalist Series*. Mark draws upon his experience and study of real estate, finance, and the wealthy to create an inspiring and most importantly effective road map to producing financial abundance in the shortest amount of time possible.

MARK MACKENZIE®
REAL ESTATE PLANNING